NE능률 영어교과서

대한민국 고등학생 **10**명 중 **4.7**명이 보는 교과서

영어 고등 교과서 점유율 1위

(7차, 2007 개정, 2009 개정, 2015 개정)

KB124619

리딩튜터

READING TUTOR

그동안 판매된
리딩튜터 1,900만 부
차곡차곡 쌓으면 19만 미터

에베레스트 21배 높이

190,000m

에베레스트 8,848m

능률보카

그동안 판매된
능률VOCA 1,100만 부

대한민국 박스오피스
천만명을 넘은 영화 단 28개

VOCA

그래머존

그동안 판매된 450만 부의 그래머존을 바닥에 쭉~ 깔면

1000km 서울-부산 왕복가능

서울

부산

교재 검토에 도움을 주신 선생님들

강건창 광주 살레시오중학교
강수정 인천 석정중학교
구영애 파주 금촌중학교
김민정 순천 엘린 영어교습소
김민정 파주 삼광중학교
김선미 천안 천안서여자중학교
김수연 서울 잉글리시아이 고덕캠퍼스
김수영 광주 숭일중학교
김연숙 서울 휘문중학교
김영현 광주 수피아여자중학교
김유빈(Annie) 동탄 애니원잉글리쉬
김현정 천안 광풍중학교
김혜원 인천 갈산중학교
나은진 서울 화곡중학교
노수정 서울 빌드업 영어교습소
문혜옥 시흥 은행중학교
민세원 광명 소하중학교
박인화 서울 일성여자중고등학교

박창현 광주 고려중학교
박혜숙 서울 경원중학교
반지혜 서울 대원국제중학교
방선영 광명 소하중학교
배영주 부산 이사벨중학교
배정현 서울 대명중학교
변재선 부천 부천중학교
서은조 서울 방배중학교
성수정 부산 주례여자중학교
신주희 서울 광성중학교
신희수 서울 이수중학교
안인숙 울산 현대중학교
양윤정 시흥 능곡고등학교
오영숙 서울 양강중학교
오하연 부산 인지중학교
오형기 서울 배문중학교
윤선경 서울 영국이엠학원
이수경 춘천 강원중학교

이임주 인천 만수북중학교
이정순 서울 일성여자중고등학교
이정재 파주 광탄중학교
이정희 천안 봉서중학교
이진영 울산 신정중학교
이효정 서울 신사중학교
장영진 광주 서강중학교
정찬희 광명 소하중학교
조혜진 성남 동광중학교
최문희 인천 삼산중학교
최수근(Claire) 광교 RISE 어학원
최은주 서울 등명중학교
최지예 대전 삼천중학교
최현우 창원 용원중학교
홍준기 광주 동신중학교
황나리 대전 덕명중학교

1316
READING LEVEL 2

지은이	NE능률 영어교육연구소
선임연구원	김지현
연구원	이지영, 김윤아, 박현영
영문교열	Patrick Ferraro, Curtis Thompson, Keeran Murphy, Angela Lan
디자인	닷츠
내지 일러스트	수지, 한상엽, 박응식
맥편집	김재민
Photo Credits	Shutterstock, Wikimedia Commons

Copyright©2024 by NE Neungyule, Inc.

All rights reserved. No part of this publication may be reproduced, stored in a retrieval system, or transmitted in any form or by any means, electronic, mechanical, photocopying, recording, or otherwise, without the prior permission of the copyright owner.

✘ 본 교재의 독창적인 내용에 대한 일체의 무단 전재 · 모방은 법률로 금지되어 있습니다.
✚ 파본은 구매처에서 교환 가능합니다.

Let's grow together

NE능률이
미래를
창조합니다.

건강한 배움의 고객가치를 제공하겠다는 꿈을 실현하기 위해
40년이 넘는 시간 동안 열심히 달려왔습니다.

앞으로도 끊임없는 연구와 노력을 통해
당연한 것을 멈추지 않고

고객, 기업, 직원 모두가 함께 성장하는 NE능률이 되겠습니다.

NE능률의 모든 교재가 한 곳에 - 엔이 북스

NE_Books

www.nebooks.co.kr ▼

NE능률의 유초등 교재부터 중고생 참고서,
토익·토플 수험서와 일반 영어까지!
PC는 물론 태블릿 PC, 스마트폰으로 언제 어디서나
NE능률의 교재와 다양한 학습 자료를 만나보세요.

✓ 필요한 부가 학습 자료 바로 찾기
✓ 주요 인기 교재들을 한눈에 확인
✓ 나에게 딱 맞는 교재를 찾아주는 스마트 검색
✓ 함께 보면 좋은 교재와 다음 단계 교재 추천
✓ 회원 가입, 교재 후기 작성 등 사이트 활동 시 NE Point 적립

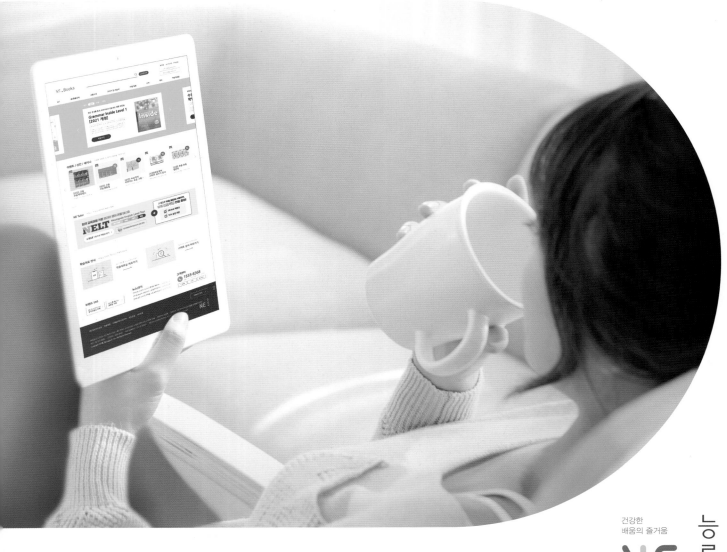

건강한
배움의 즐거움
NE 능률

영어교과서 리딩튜터 능률보카 빠른독해 바른독해 수능만만 월등한 개념 수학 유형더블
NE_Build & Grow   NE_Times   NE_Kids(굿잡,상상수프)   NE_능률 주니어랩   아이챌린지

기초부터 내신까지 중학 독해 완성

1316

1316 READING

LEVEL
2

STRUCTURE & FEATURES

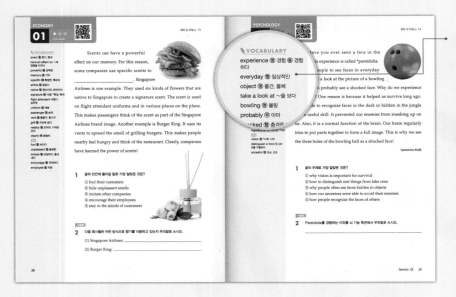

VOCABULARY

지문과 문제에 나오는 중요 단어의
의미를 확인해 볼 수 있습니다.
먼저 지문을 읽으면서 모르는 단어의
의미를 추론해 보고, 그 뜻이 맞는지
확인해 보세요.

유익하고 다채로운 지문

문화, 과학, 예술, 역사 등 약 20가지에
이르는 다양한 분야의 재미있고
유익한 정보를 담은 40개의 지문을
엄선했습니다.

ONE-PAGE READING

각 Section의 첫 번째, 두 번째 지문은
단문 독해 코너로, 짧은 글을 읽으며
비교적 간단한 문제를 풀어 보고,
부담 없이 영문 독해를 연습할 수 있습니다.

REVIEW TEST

각 Section의 마무리 코너로 Review Test
가 있습니다. 앞의 지문에서 배운 어휘와 숙어
를 다시 확인해 보세요. 다양한 유형의 문제들
로 어휘 응용력을 높일 수 있습니다.

WORKBOOK

각 지문에 대한 주요 어휘 및 핵심 구문을 복습
할 수 있도록 지문별 연습 문제를 제공합니다.
모든 문제가 지문 내용을 기반으로 출제되어
어려움 없이 복습이 가능합니다.

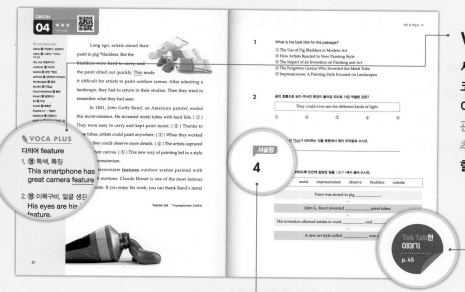

VOCA PLUS

세 번째, 네 번째 지문에만 제공되는 코너로, 지문에 나온 단어 중 주요 어휘를 골라 다의어, 접두사/접미사, 관련 어휘, 형태가 비슷한 어휘들을 추가로 수록하여 체계적인 단어 학습을 할 수 있습니다.

TWO-PAGE READING

각 Section의 세 번째, 네 번째 지문은 독해 실력을 한층 더 높일 수 있는 장문 독해 코너입니다. 이 지문들을 통해 긴 지문에 대한 두려움을 없애 보세요. 또한, 각 지문에 하나씩 있는 영어 지시문 문제를 통해 영어에 대한 자신감을 높일 수 있습니다.

다양한 서술형 문항

최근 내신 출제 경향을 반영한 다양한 서술형 문제들로 중등 내신에 완벽하게 대비할 수 있습니다.
도표 및 요약문을 완성하는 문제들을 제공하여 지문을 체계적으로 이해하는 데 도움을 줍니다.

TALK TALK한 이야기

2개의 장문 독해 중 하나는 Section 마지막 페이지의 〈Talk Talk한 이야기〉와 연결되어 있습니다. 마지막 문제 아래에 태그가 있는지 찾아보세요.
Talk Talk한 이야기에서는 지문과 관련된 배경지식 및 일반 상식들을 부담 없는 분량으로 담았습니다. 잠시 머리를 식힐 겸 가볍게 읽어 보세요. 여러분의 상식이 더 넓어질 거예요!

CONTENTS

Section

1

✎ VOCABULARY

conversation 명 대화
confused 형 혼란스러워하는
and so on 기타 등등, ~ 등
be made up of ~으로 구성
되다
phrase 명 *구(句); 구절
sentence 명 문장
capitalize 동 대문자로 쓰다
commonly 부 흔히, 보통
type 명 유형 *동 타자 치다
fit into ~에 꼭 들어맞다
release 동 발표하다, 공개하다

Look at the conversation on the phone. Are you confused by the words *TBH*, *GOAT*, and so on? These words are *acronyms. Acronyms are made up of the first letters of the words in a phrase or a sentence. That's why they are all capitalized. For example, the acronym of "to be honest" is TBH. Acronyms are commonly used online and in text messages. They make it easy to type short messages. Now try reading the conversation again!

*acronym 두문자어(각 단어의 첫 글자로 만든 말)

> Who is your favorite singer?
>
> TBH, I like Bruno Mars. He is the GOAT.
>
> He is super cool! BTW, did you listen to his new song?
>
> Oh, I forgot it was released today!
>
> IMO, you should listen to it RN.
>
> Okay, BRB.

GOAT = greatest of all time
BTW = by the way
IMO = _____ _____ _____
RN = right now
BRB = be right back

서술형

1 사람들이 온라인에서 두문자어를 사용하는 이유를 본문에서 찾아 우리말로 쓰시오.

_____

2 빈칸에 알맞은 말을 | 보기 |에서 골라 쓰시오.

| 보기 | in my office   in my opinion   in memory of |

IMO = _____ _____ _____

8

SCIENCE
02
★ ☆ ☆
108 words

VOCABULARY

soda 몡 탄산음료
bump 몡 튀어나온 부분, 돌기
bottom 몡 맨 아래 (부분),
바닥
contain 통 들어 있다, 포함
하다
pressure 몡 압력
inside 젠 ~의 안에
resist 통 저항하다
area 몡 지역; *면적
increase 통 증가시키다,
늘리다
spread out 널리 퍼지다
outward 부 바깥쪽으로,
밖으로
balance 몡 균형
eventually 부 결국
fall over 넘어지다
문제
solution 몡 해결책

Plastic soda bottles have five bumps on the bottom. However, you won't find them on plastic bottles that contain water or juice. Why is this? It's because soda has *carbon dioxide in it. This gas creates a lot of pressure inside the plastic bottle. The bottle must be able to resist this pressure. If the bottle has a greater area, there will be less pressure in it. That's why the bumps are added. They increase the area of the bottle and spread the pressure out. What would happen without the bumps? The pressure would push the bottom outward. Then the bottle would lose balance and eventually fall over.

*carbon dioxide 이산화탄소

---

1 글의 내용과 일치하지 <u>않는</u> 것은?

① 물이 담긴 페트병의 바닥면은 주로 평평하다.
② 탄산음료가 담긴 페트병의 내부 압력은 매우 크다.
③ 페트병의 면적이 클수록 내부 압력은 작아진다.
④ 페트병 바닥의 돌기들은 내부 압력을 높인다.
⑤ 바닥이 평평한 페트병에 탄산음료를 넣으면 그 병은 넘어질 것이다.

서술형

2 글의 내용과 일치하도록 빈칸에 알맞은 말을 본문에서 찾아 쓰시오.

Problem	Carbon dioxide in soda bottles produces _____, which pushes the bottom out and causes them to fall over.
Solution	_____ were added to the bottom of the soda bottles.

📖 VOCABULARY

underwater 🕮 물속에서
🕮 수중의

device 🕮 (기계적) 장치

shape 🕮 모양, 형태
*🕮 ~의 모양을 이루다

breathe 🕮 호흡하다, 숨 쉬다

species 🕮 (생물의) 종(種)

web 🕮 거미줄[집]

surface 🕮 표면, 수면

belly 🕮 배, 복부

trap 🕮 가두다

release 🕮 놓아 주다

leak out 새어 나오다

gather 🕮 모으다

문제
maintain 🕮 유지하다

particular 🕮 특정한

📖 VOCA PLUS

다의어 cover

1. 🕮 (감추기 위해) 씌우다
   [가리다]
   He covered his mouth
   with his hands.

2. 🕮 덮다
   Snow covered the
   whole mountain.

3. 🕮 덮개, 커버
   a pillow cover

4. 🕮 (책 등의) 표지
   I like the cover of the
   book.

In the past, people used *diving bells to go underwater. These devices were shaped like a bell and held air for divers to breathe. In nature, the diving bell spider makes its own diving bell. It is the only species of spider that spends its whole life underwater. First, it makes an underwater web between plants. Then it _____(A)_____ air bubbles from the surface using its legs and belly. These body parts are covered in hairs. The hairs help trap the bubbles. The spider brings these bubbles to the web and releases them. It _____(B)_____ this process until the bubble is big enough to live in. Over time, air leaks out, and the spider must gather more bubbles. It spends most of its life living inside its bubble house.

*diving bell 잠수종(사람을 태워 물 속 깊이 내려 보낼 때 쓰는 잠수 기구)

1 다음 중 글에서 언급된 내용이 <u>아닌</u> 것은? (2가지)

① how long the bubbles last
② why the spider lives underwater
③ how long the spider stays underwater
④ how the spider makes its home
⑤ what the spider has on its legs

2 글의 빈칸 (A)와 (B)에 들어갈 말이 알맞게 짝지어진 것은?

	(A)		(B)
①	collects	⋯⋯	provides
②	collects	⋯⋯	repeats
③	produces	⋯⋯	repeats
④	produces	⋯⋯	provides
⑤	builds	⋯⋯	repeats

서술형

3 다음 질문에 대한 답을 본문에서 찾아 우리말로 간단히 쓰시오.

> How does the spider maintain its home?

_____

서술형

4 다음 영영 뜻풀이에 해당하는 단어를 본문에서 찾아 쓰시오.

> to keep something in a particular place, especially if it is useful

_____

Talk Talk**한**
이야기
⋯⋯⋯⋯⋯
p. 15

✎ VOCABULARY

pay for 대금을 지불하다
probably (円) 아마도
trade (동) 교환하다 (명) 물물
교환
paper clip 종이 끼우는 클립
impressed (형) 감명을 받은
exchange A for B A를
B로 바꾸다
a pair of 한 쌍의 ~
earring (명) 귀걸이
glass (명) 유리; *(pl.) 안경
vacuum cleaner 진공
청소기
post (동) (글을) 게시하다
attention (명) 주목; *관심
border (명) 국경

✎ VOCA PLUS

동사 + -able → 형용사
┌ value (동) 소중하게 여기다
└ valuable (형) 귀중한; 가치가
  큰, 값비싼
┌ believe (동) 믿다
└ believable (형) 믿을 수 있는
┌ comfort (동) 위로[위안]하다
└ comfortable (형) 편안한

Is it possible to pay for a new house with a hairpin? You probably think it isn't. But that's what an American woman named Demi Skipper did. One day, she watched a man's TED Talk. He traded up from a paper clip to a house. She was greatly impressed and decided to try the same thing. First, she exchanged a hairpin for a pair of earrings. She then traded the earrings for four glasses. Next, the glasses became a vacuum cleaner! However, as the items became more valuable, it became harder to find trading partners. So Skipper posted her story on social media. It got lots of attention. As a result, she was able to make 28 trades in 18 months, although she had a problem with her 27th trade. The trade was for a truck from a Canadian. But it was hard to bring it across the border. 그녀가 그것을 미국으로 들여오는 데 5개월이 걸렸다. Finally, Skipper made her last trade. She exchanged the truck for a house!

1   Skipper의 물물 교환에 관한 설명 중 글의 내용과 일치하는 것은?

① 종이를 끼우는 클립으로 물물 교환을 시작했다.
② 귀걸이를 진공청소기와 바꾸었다.
③ 거래하는 물건의 크기가 클수록 많은 관심을 받았다.
④ 미국 내에서만 총 28번의 물물 교환을 했다.
⑤ 27번째 물물 교환을 완료하는 데 오랜 시간이 걸렸다.

2   글의 밑줄 친 우리말을 바르게 영작한 것은?

① It took five months for her getting it into the US.
② It took five months of her to get it into the US.
③ It took five months by her to get it into the US.
④ It took five months for her to get it into the US.
⑤ It took five months by her getting it into the US.

서술형

3   다음 질문에 대한 답을 본문에서 찾아 우리말로 쓰시오.

> What did Skipper do to find trading partners?

_____

서술형

4   Skipper가 집을 구매하기까지 거래해 온 물건들을 본문에서 찾아 영어로 쓰시오.

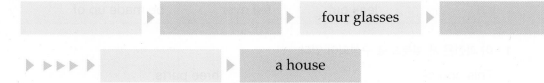

four glasses

a house

REVIEW TEST

정답 및 해설 p. 5

A 다음 의미에 해당하는 단어를 | 보기 |에서 찾아 쓰시오.

| 보기 |　　maintain　　resist　　border　　confused　　attention

1 _____ : unable to understand something

2 _____ : to keep something in good condition

3 _____ : the interest that people give to something

4 _____ : the line that separates two countries

5 _____ : to remain strong against the effect or force of something

B 다음 밑줄 친 단어와 의미가 반대되는 것을 고르시오.

1 His hobby is collecting <u>valuable</u> pictures.

① priceless　　② famous　　③ tiny　　④ precious　　⑤ worthless

2 I need to <u>gather</u> information about the topic on the internet.

① search　　② collect　　③ increase　　④ provide　　⑤ spread

3 This area is <u>commonly</u> visited by young people.

① rarely　　② often　　③ always　　④ usually　　⑤ quickly

C 우리말과 같은 뜻이 되도록 빈칸에 들어갈 말을 | 보기 |에서 골라 알맞은 형태로 쓰시오.

| 보기 |　　　　leak out　　fall over　　be made up of

1 이 과정은 세 부분으로 구성되어 있다.

This course _____ three parts.

2 나는 넘어져서 무릎을 다쳤다.

I _____ and hurt my knee.

3 금이 간 벽에서 물이 새어 나온다.

The water _____ from the cracked wall.

세계의 신기하고 희귀한 거미들

개 머리 or 토끼 머리?

어느 날 사진작가 안드레아스 케이(Andreas Kay)는 아마존 숲에서 사진을 찍다가 특이한 거미를 발견했어요. 몸통이 마치 개의 머리처럼 생긴 거미였죠. 몸통 앞쪽에 있는 검은 두 눈은 개의 콧구멍 같았어요. 이 거미는 바로 메타그린 비콜럼나타(Metagryne bicolumnata)예요. 몸에 비해 긴 다리가 특징이며, 대체로 사람 손톱만한 크기죠. 독이 없으며, 잡식성으로 알려져 있어요. 해외에서는 토끼처럼 생겼다며 Bunny Harvestman(토끼 장님 거미)라고도 불려요.

내 엉덩이는 무적 방패

특이하게 생긴 이 거미는 시클로코스미아(Cyclocosmia)예요. 방패거미 또는 도장거미라고도 불려요. 잘린 듯한 엉덩이 쪽에 특이한 무늬가 있어서 붙여진 이름이죠. 시클로코스미아는 땅속에 7~15 센티미터 정도의 구멍을 판 다음 엉덩이로 구멍을 막아요. 딱딱한 엉덩이가 자신을 방어하는 역할을 해주죠. 땅굴을 파고 그 안에 잠복해 있다가 사냥하는 것으로 알려져 있어요. 주로 중국 남동부와 인도 차이나 반도에 서식하며 다행히 독성은 없다고 해요.

곤충계의 패셔니스타

조류계에 극락조가 있다면 곤충계에는 공작새거미가 있다! 정식 명칭은 마라투스(Maratus)로 호주 고유종이죠. 보통 5 밀리미터 정도의 길이로, 수컷의 구애춤이 특히 유명해요. 암컷을 유혹하기 위해 화려한 색과 무늬를 과시하고 배를 진동시키죠. 암컷이 관심을 보이면 짝짓기를 하지만 관심이 없는데도 눈치 없이 춤을 추면 암컷은 수컷을 잡아먹기도 해요. 주로 곤충과 다른 거미를 잡아먹고, 예리한 시력을 사용해 먹이를 찾는 것으로 알려져 있죠. 색이 정말 화려하지 않나요?

Section

2

ACTIVITIES

01
★☆☆
105 words

📖 VOCABULARY

deadline ⑲ 마감 시간, 기한
meet ⑧ 만나다; *(기한 등을) 지키다
fill out ~을 작성하다
form ⑲ 양식
pressure ⑲ 압력, 압박
mild ⑲ 가벼운
staff ⑲ 직원
progress ⑲ 진행
normal ⑲ 보통의
hourly ⑨ 시간마다
below ⑨ 아래에
provide ⑧ 제공하다
available ⑲ 이용할 수 있는
unlimited ⑲ 무제한의
cost ⑧ (비용이) ~이다
afterward ⑨ 그 후에
문제
essay ⑲ 과제물, 리포트

Do you have a deadline to meet? The Deadline Café can help! When you enter, you fill out a form with your name, your work goal, and the time you need. You also choose the amount of pressure you want. With "mild," the staff will only check your progress before you leave. "Normal" means they will check it hourly. And with "hard," they will keep watching you until you finish your work. See below for more information.

☑ Free Wi-Fi is provided.
☑ Only fifteen seats are available.
☑ Coffee and tea are self-serve and unlimited.
☑ The first thirty minutes cost $1 and each hour afterward costs $2.50.

1 The Deadline Café에 대한 설명 중 글의 내용과 일치하지 <u>않는</u> 것은?

① 입장할 때 목표 작업량을 적어야 한다.
② 'normal'을 선택하면 직원이 매시간 진행 상황을 확인한다.
③ 와이파이를 무료로 사용할 수 있다.
④ 총 좌석 수가 15개이며 예약이 필요하다.
⑤ 커피와 차가 무제한으로 제공된다.

서술형

2 다음 양식을 보고 Emily가 지불해야 할 금액을 쓰시오.

$ _____

Name: Emily	Pressure: mild
Start: 2:00	Finish: 4:30
Work Goal: finish an essay	

18

SCIENCE
02
★ ☆ ☆
107 words

VOCABULARY

calm 형 고요한

peaceful 형 평화로운

snowflake 명 눈송이

side 명 쪽, 면; *(도형의) 변

empty 형 빈, 비어 있는

space 명 *공간; 우주

absorb 동 흡수하다

sound wave 음파

nearby 형 인근의, 가까운 곳의

melt 동 녹다

freeze 동 얼다

completely 부 완전히

ability 명 능력

icy 형 얼음의, 얼음에 뒤덮인

surface 명 표면

reflect 동 반사하다

instead 부 그 대신에

actually 부 실제로

disappear 동 사라지다

문제

movement 명 움직임

temperature 명 온도, 기온

Why do snowy nights seem so calm and peaceful? It's because snow makes everything quieter! The _____ of snowflakes makes this possible. They have six sides. Each side has lots of empty spaces. These spaces absorb sound waves. As a result, everything nearby becomes quieter. As the snow melts, the spaces in the snowflakes get smaller. This changes the shape of the snowflakes. When the melting snow freezes again, the snowflakes completely lose their special ability. They become an icy surface and reflect sound waves instead. This actually makes sounds seem louder. So enjoy snowy nights. When the snow starts to melt, the special feeling will disappear.

1 글의 빈칸에 들어갈 말로 가장 알맞은 것은?

① size
② shape
③ number
④ movement
⑤ temperature

서술형

2 글의 밑줄 친 their special ability가 의미하는 것을 우리말로 쓰시오.

_____

VOCABULARY

unique 형 고유의; 독특한
symbol 명 상징
arrow 명 화살표
letter 명 편지; *글자
look like ~처럼 보이다
customer 명 고객
dot 명 점
represent 동 나타내다,
의미하다
original 형 원래의, 본래의

VOCA PLUS

다의어 store

1. 명 가게, 상점
   My brother bought
   candies at a store.

2. 동 저장하다, 보관하다
   Store fruits in a dry
   place.

A logo is the unique symbol of a company. Through its logo, a company shows ⓐ what it is. One example comes from Amazon, a famous online shopping company. Its logo is its name in *lowercase and an orange arrow. The arrow has two meanings. First, the arrow starts at the letter *a* and ⓑ end at the letter *z*. This shows that Amazon sells everything. Second, the arrow is ⓒ curved, so it looks like a smile. This means that Amazon wants to make customers ⓓ happy.

Domino's, the largest pizza company in the world, also has a unique logo. The Domino's logo has a domino with three dots on ⓔ it. The dots represent the company's original three stores. At first, Domino's wanted to add a dot for every new store. However, the company changed its mind. That was a good decision, because there are now about 20,000 stores!

*lowercase 소문자

1   What is the best title for the passage?

    ① How Companies Make Their Logos
    ② The Most Famous Logos Ever Created
    ③ How Logos Affect the Sales of Companies
    ④ The Hidden Meanings behind Famous Logos
    ⑤ The Difficulty of Making Unique Logos

2   글의 밑줄 친 ⓐ~ⓔ중 어법상 어색한 것은?

    ① ⓐ   ② ⓑ   ③ ⓒ   ④ ⓓ   ⑤ ⓔ

3   글에서 묘사하는 Amazon의 로고에 가장 가까운 것은?

    ① **Amazon**   ② **amazon**
    ③ **amazon**   ④ **amazon**
    ⑤ **Amazon**

서술형

4   Domino's의 로고에 있는 세 개의 점은 무엇을 나타내는지 본문에서 찾아 영어로 쓰시오. (5단어)

    _____

❧ VOCABULARY

creation 명 창조, 창작
run 동 달리다; *운영하다
dish 명 접시; *요리
guest 명 손님
tender 형 부드러운
come up with ~을 생각해
내다, 떠올리다
dough 명 반죽
flip 동 휙 뒤집다
upside down 거꾸로
serve 동 (음식을) 제공하다
bottom 명 맨 아래; *바닥
customer 명 손님, 고객
start over 다시 시작하다
absorb 동 흡수하다, 빨아들
이다
rich 형 부유한; *(맛·향이) 진한,
풍부한
문제
slight 형 약간의, 사소한
complaint 명 불평
unfortunate 형 불운한,
불행한

❧ VOCA PLUS

형태가 비슷한 어휘
lay (lay-laid-laid)
1. 동 놓다, 눕히다
   I laid the baby on the
   bed.

2. (알을) 낳다
   Chickens lay eggs.

lie
1. 동 눕다, 누워 있다
   (lie-lay-lain)
   Lie on your back,
   please.

2. 동 거짓말하다
   (lie-lied-lied) 명 거짓말
   You must not lie.
   white lie

_____ led to Stéphanie Tatin's creation of a delicious dessert. In the 1880s, Stéphanie ran a hotel with her sister in France. Stéphanie worked as a chef in the hotel. Her best dish was an apple tart. Her tart was a big hit with hotel guests, as it was tender and sweet.

(A) Then she came up with a bright idea. She simply put the dough on top of the sliced apples! When it was baked, she just flipped the tart upside down and served it.

(B) One day, Stéphanie was busy and forgot about the tart dough. She had only laid apple slices with sugar in the bottom of the pan! But many customers were waiting for the dish, so she couldn't start over.

(C) Baking it in this way helped the apples absorb the sugar better. Stéphanie's new tart tasted richer and sweeter than ever! That was the moment tarte Tatin was born.

1 What is the best choice for the blank?

① A stolen recipe
② A slight mistake
③ A perfect plan
④ A complaint by a customer
⑤ An unfortunate accident

2 (A)~(C)를 글의 흐름에 알맞게 배열한 것은?

① (A) — (B) — (C)   ② (A) — (C) — (B)
③ (B) — (A) — (C)   ④ (B) — (C) — (A)
⑤ (C) — (B) — (A)

서술형

3 글의 밑줄 친 a bright idea가 의미하는 것을 본문에서 찾아 우리말로 쓰시오.

_____

서술형

4 다음 영영 뜻풀이에 해당하는 단어를 본문에서 찾아 쓰시오.

the act of making something new

_____

Talk Talk**한**
이야기
·············
p. 25

REVIEW TEST

정답 및 해설 p. 8

A 다음 의미에 해당하는 단어를 | 보기 |에서 찾아 쓰시오.

| | 보기 | serve   tender   symbol   surface   disappear |

1 _____ : a picture used to represent something

2 _____ : offer someone food or drink

3 _____ : the top part or outside of something

4 _____ : to move out of view

5 _____ : soft and easy to chew

B 다음 밑줄 친 단어와 의미가 반대되는 것을 고르시오.

1 The ship sank to the <u>bottom</u> of the ocean.
  ① side　　　② middle　　　③ top　　　④ floor　　　⑤ pressure

2 I want a <u>calm</u> place for my vacation.
  ① quiet　　　② tiny　　　③ large　　　④ noisy　　　⑤ peaceful

3 Write your name in the blank <u>below</u>.
  ① high　　　② above　　　③ afterward　　　④ under　　　⑤ behind

C 우리말과 같은 뜻이 되도록 빈칸에 들어갈 말을 | 보기 |에서 골라 알맞은 형태로 쓰시오.

| | 보기 | fill out   look like   come up with |

1 그 고양이 인형은 호랑이처럼 보인다.
  The cat doll _____ a tiger.

2 어떻게 이런 기발한 생각을 했니?
  How did you _____ this brilliant idea?

3 너는 이 신청서를 작성해야 한다.
  You should _____ this application form.

Talk Talk한 이야기

예기치 않게
만들어진 음식들

세상에는 Tatin Tart(타탱 타르트)처럼 예기치 않은 사건이나 실수로 더 좋은 음식을 발명하거나, 만들어 낸 여러 가지 사건들이 있습니다. 또 어떤 것들이 있는지 알아볼까요?

초콜릿케이크에서 실수로 태어난 브라우니 (brownie)

브라우니 탄생 비화는 여러 이야기로 전해지고 있는데요. 그중 타탱 타르트 이야기와 비슷한 것을 소개합니다. 미국 팔머 하우스 호텔(the Palmer House Hotel)의 제빵사가 초콜릿케이크로 만들 반죽을 하다가 그만 베이킹파우더를 넣는 것을 깜빡 잊고 맙니다. 선택의 여지가 없었던 제빵사는 그대로 반죽을 오븐에 넣었더니 단단하고 부풀지 않은 상태의 초콜릿케이크가 되었습니다. 이 케이크는 곧 팔머 호텔의 대표적인 디저트, 즉 브라우니의 시초가 되었습니다.

짓궂은 장난으로 탄생한 감자칩 (potato chips)

전 세계적으로 인기 있는 과자인 감자칩은 1853년 요리사 조지 크럼(George Crum)이 우연히 발명한 것으로 알려져 있습니다. 뉴욕의 한 고급 식당에서 손님 중 한 명이 감자튀김이 너무 두껍고, 바삭하지 않다고 불평했습니다. 크럼은 감자튀김을 포크로 찍어 먹지 못하게 종이처럼 얇게 썰어서 바싹 튀겨 주었는데, 이 손님이 얇은 감자튀김을 맛있게 먹으면서 최초의 감자칩이 탄생하게 되었답니다.

11세 소년이 만든 아이스바, 팝시클 (popsicle)

1905년, 샌프란시스코의 프랭크 에퍼슨(Frank Epperson)이라는 11세의 소년이 집에서 직접 음료를 만들었습니다. 그것은 소다 가루에 찬물을 섞은 것이었는데, 소년은 만들던 음료를 채 완성하지 못하고 뒷문 밖에 두고 깜빡 잊어버렸습니다. 밤사이에 눈이 내렸고, 그다음 날이 되자 음료는 휘젓기 위해 병에 담가 둔 나무 막대와 함께 얼어 있었습니다. 이것이 바로 최초의 팝시클입니다.

Section

3

VOCABULARY

sidewalk 명 보도, 인도
harm 동 해를 끼치다, 손상시키다
contain 동 ~이 들어 있다, 포함하다
chemical 명 화학 물질
soil 명 토양, 흙
cause 동 야기하다, 초래하다
flow 동 흐르다
stream 명 개울, 시내
heating wire 전열선
melt 동 녹이다
volcanic 형 화산의
mineral 명 *광물(질); 무기물
prevent 동 막다, 방지하다
slide 동 미끄러지다
slippery 형 미끄러운
harmless 형 해가 없는, 무해한

문제
alternative 명 대안

*De-icing products allow us to safely walk on sidewalks and drive on roads after winter storms. However, they harm the environment. (①) They contain chemicals that are bad for the soil. (②) These chemicals can also cause problems for fish if they flow into lakes and streams. (③) One example is a type of road with heating wires that can melt snow and ice. (④) Another example is **Ecotraction. (⑤) It is made from volcanic minerals. It prevents people and cars from sliding on slippery roads. And it is harmless to the environment!

*de-icing 얼음을 제거하는, 제설의
**Ecotraction 에코트랙션(친환경 마찰제)

1 글의 주제로 가장 알맞은 것은?

① 제설제의 이점
② 친환경적인 제설제 대체품
③ 눈길 교통사고를 막는 방법
④ 화산재의 뛰어난 제설 효과
⑤ 제설제가 환경에 악영향을 주는 이유

2 글의 흐름으로 보아 주어진 문장이 들어갈 위치로 가장 적절한 곳은?

Fortunately, people have made alternatives to these harmful chemicals.

① ② ③ ④ ⑤

PSYCHOLOGY

02
★ ☆ ☆
101 words

✎ VOCABULARY

imagine ⑧ 상상하다
expensive ⑧ 비싼
pretty ⑨ 어느 정도, 꽤
cheap ⑧ (값이) 싼
experience ⑧ 경험하다
effect ⑨ 영향; *효과
occur ⑧ 일어나다, 발생하다
make a decision 결정을 내리다
based on ~에 근거하여
receive ⑧ 받다
in other words 다시 말해서, 즉
discounted ⑧ 할인된
above ⑳ ~보다 위에
original ⑧ 원래의, 본래의
as a result 결과적으로
consumer ⑨ 고객, 소비자
make money 돈을 벌다

Imagine you go shopping and find cool shoes for $150. You think they are too expensive. Next, you see different shoes for $80. You think they're pretty cheap, so you buy them. You have just experienced the anchoring effect! The anchoring effect occurs when people make decisions based on the first information they receive. In other words, they become "*anchored" to this information. Stores often use the anchoring effect by showing the discounted price above the original price. It (seem, discounted, better, makes, the, price). As a result, consumers are more likely to buy the item, and stores make more money.

*anchored 닻을 내린

1 글의 주제로 가장 알맞은 것은?

① 물건을 싸게 잘 사는 방법
② 고객이 물건을 사도록 유도하는 방법
③ 상점들이 그들의 제품을 광고하는 방법
④ 충동구매를 피하고 돈을 절약하는 방법
⑤ 상점들이 제품의 할인가를 결정하는 방법

서술형

2 글의 ( ) 안에 주어진 단어를 바르게 배열하여 문장을 완성하시오.

_____

VOCABULARY

albinism 명 백색증, 색소 결핍증
uncommon 형 흔하지 않은
condition 명 상태; *질환, 병
affect 동 영향을 미치다; 병이 나게 하다
feather 명 깃털
as well 또한, 역시
nutrient 명 영양분
albino 형 백색증을 가진
redwood 명 삼나무
survive 동 살아남다
attach 동 붙이다, 접착하다
root 명 뿌리
parasite 명 기생충
remove 동 제거하다, 없애다
문제
toxic 형 유독성의
substance 명 물질

VOCA PLUS

다의어 plant
1. 명 식물, 초목
   Plants need water to grow.
2. 명 공장
   A power plant produces electricity.
3. 동 (씨앗 등을) 심다
   I planted a sunflower in my garden.

Albinism is an uncommon condition. It affects both people and animals. It causes them to have white skin, hair, and feathers. They might also have pink or blue eyes. Surprisingly, plants can be affected by albinism as well!

Plants with albinism don't have any *chlorophyll, which helps plants make nutrients. For this reason, most albino plants have short lives. Redwood trees, however, are different. There are many albino redwoods in California. They have white leaves that turn brown in winter. The albino redwoods survive by attaching their roots to the roots of other trees. This allows them to get the nutrients they need.

You may think these trees are parasites because they take nutrients from the trees around them. But the albino redwoods help the other trees, too. They remove **toxins from the soil. As a result, all of the trees in the area can survive.

*chlorophyll 엽록소 **toxin 독소

1 What is this passage mainly about?

① why albinism occurs in plants
② why chlorophyll is important to plants
③ why most albino plants live in California
④ how albino redwoods survive in nature
⑤ how albino redwoods differ from other redwoods

2 Albinism에 대한 설명 중 글의 내용과 일치하는 것은?

① 사람과 동물에게만 발생하는 희귀병이다.
② 이 병에 걸린 식물들은 보통 긴 수명을 가졌다.
③ 이 병에 걸린 삼나무의 잎은 사계절 하얀색을 띤다.
④ 이 병에 걸린 삼나무는 다른 식물로부터 양분을 얻는다.
⑤ 이 병에 걸린 삼나무는 유독한 물질을 토양으로 배출한다.

서술형

3 Albinism이 인간과 동물에게 어떤 영향을 미치는지 본문에서 찾아 우리말로 쓰시오. (2가지)

(1) _____

(2) _____

서술형

4 글의 내용과 일치하도록 빈칸에 알맞은 말을 | 보기 |에서 골라 쓰시오.

| 보기 | disease   producing   nutrients   removing   parasites

Albino redwoods are often thought as _____ because they get _____ by attaching their roots to the roots of nearby trees. But they also help these other trees by _____ toxic substances from the soil.

Talk Talk한
이야기
p. 35

✎ **VOCABULARY**

store 통 저장하다, 보관하다
carry 통 나르다; *가지고 다니다
dry out 메말라지다
outdoor 형 야외의
scene 명 장면; *풍경
admire 통 감탄하며 바라보다
landscape 명 풍경
studio 명 작업실
inconvenience 명 불편
invent 통 발명하다
lid 명 뚜껑
moist 형 촉촉한
thanks to ~ 덕분에
observe 통 관찰하다
capture 통 붙잡다, *(사진·글 등으로) 담아내다
rapid 형 빠른
motion 명 움직임
문제
modern 형 현대의
react 통 반응하다
forgotten 형 잊혀진

✎ **VOCA PLUS**

다의어 feature
1. 명 특색, 특징
   This smartphone has a great camera feature.

2. 명 이목구비, 얼굴 생김새
   His eyes are his best feature.

3. 통 특징으로 삼다, 특별히 포함하다
   The gym features a pool.

Long ago, artists stored their paint in pig *bladders. But the bladders were hard to carry, and the paint dried out quickly. This made it difficult for artists to paint outdoor scenes. After admiring a landscape, they had to return to their studios. Then they tried to remember what they had seen.

In 1841, John Goffe Rand, an American painter, ended this inconvenience. He invented metal tubes with hard lids. (①) They were easy to carry and kept paint moist. (②) Thanks to these tubes, artists could paint anywhere. (③) When they worked outside, they could observe more details. (④) The artists captured them on their canvas. (⑤) This new way of painting led to a style called **impressionism.

Impressionism features outdoor scenes painted with rapid brush motions. Claude Monet is one of the most famous impressionists. If you enjoy his work, you can thank Rand's metal tubes.

*bladder 방광 **impressionism 인상주의

32

1   What is the best title for the passage?

① The Use of Pig Bladders in Modern Art
② How Artists Reacted to New Painting Style
③ The Impact of an Invention on Painting and Art
④ The Forgotten Genius Who Invented the Metal Tube
⑤ Impressionism: A Painting Style Focused on Landscapes

2   글의 흐름으로 보아 주어진 문장이 들어갈 위치로 가장 적절한 곳은?

> They could even see the different kinds of light.

①   ②   ③   ④   ⑤

서술형

3   글의 밑줄 친 <u>This</u>가 의미하는 것을 본문에서 찾아 우리말로 쓰시오.

_____

서술형

4   글의 내용과 일치하도록 빈칸에 알맞은 말을 | 보기 |에서 골라 쓰시오.

| 보기 | metal   impressionism   observe   bladders   outside

Paint was stored in pig _____.

▼

John G. Rand invented _____ paint tubes.

▼

His invention allowed artists to work _____ and _____ more details.

▼

A new art style called _____ was created.

A 다음 의미에 해당하는 단어를 | 보기 |에서 찾아 쓰시오.

| 보기 |　　　flow　　　nutrient　　　remove　　　cheap　　　slippery

1 _____ : difficult to hold or to move on because it is smooth or wet

2 _____ : to take something away from a place

3 _____ : a substance that living things need to live and grow

4 _____ : to keep moving in one direction

5 _____ : costing less than you expected

B 다음 밑줄 친 단어와 의미가 비슷한 것을 고르시오.

1 He took a picture of the beautiful <u>landscape</u>.

① nature　　② scenery　　③ sign　　④ desert　　⑤ detail

2 My grandfather made a <u>rapid</u> recovery.

① slow　　② quiet　　③ quick　　④ moist　　⑤ huge

3 This cleaning product is <u>harmless</u> to children.

① safe　　② useless　　③ helpful　　④ dangerous　　⑤ important

C 우리말과 같은 뜻이 되도록 빈칸에 들어갈 말을 | 보기 |에서 골라 알맞은 형태로 쓰시오.

| 보기 |　　　thanks to　　　as well　　　based on

1 그녀는 춤 또한 잘 춘다.

She is good at dancing _____.

2 이것은 실제 사건들에 기반을 둔 소설이다.

This is a novel _____ real-life events.

3 당신 덕분에 내가 지갑을 찾았다.

_____ you, I found my wallet.

우리는 윈윈 관계

백색증에 걸린 삼나무도 다른 나무들에 기생하지만 도움을 주기도 하잖아. 자연에서는 이렇게 주고 받는 경우가 은근히 많은 것 같아.

그런 걸 윈윈(win-win)이라고 하잖아. 새우랑 고비(goby) 물고기도 그 중 하나야. 새우가 시력이 무척 나빠서 앞을 잘 볼 수 없는데, 고비 물고기가 보디가드(bodyguard)가 되어 주거든.

어떻게 보호해 주는데?

고비 물고기는 시력이 좋아서 새우의 눈 역할을 해 주고, 천적이 다가올 때 꼬리를 쳐서 새우에게 위험하다고 알려 줘.

새우는 이렇게 고비 물고기의 몸에 붙어 있다가 위험 신호를 받자마자 바닷속 모랫구멍으로 쏙 들어가지!

와 정말 딱 붙어 다니네. 귀엽다. 😊
새우에게 고비 물고기는 꼭 필요한 존재구나!

맞아. 하지만 고비 물고기에게도 새우가 중요한 존재야.
고비 물고기는 크기가 작기 때문에 혼자서 모랫구멍을 팔 수도 집을 지을 수도 없어.

집을 지을 때는 새우가 고비 물고기를 도와주니?

응. 새우가 모랫구멍을 파서 고비 물고기와 함께 살 집을 마련하지. 구멍 속의 이물질과 모래들을 온종일 청소하는 게 새우의 역할이야. 가끔 새우가 모랫구멍에서 멀리 나갔을 때면 고비 물고기가 새우를 다시 찾아온대.

고비 물고기를 위해 모랫구멍을 파내는 새우와 새우를 천적으로부터 지켜주는 고비 물고기라니....
서로에게 윈윈 맞네!

www.nebooks.co.kr

Section

4

ECONOMY

01

★ ☆ ☆
110 words

VOCABULARY

scent ⑲ 향기, 향내

have an effect on ~에 영향을 미치다

powerful ⑲ 강력한

memory ⑲ 기억

specific ⑲ 특정한, 특유의

airline ⑲ 항공사

native ⑲ 원산지의, 토박이의

signature ⑲ 서명; *특징, 특색

flight attendant 비행기 승무원

uniform ⑲ 제복

passenger ⑲ 승객

vent ⑲ 통풍구, 환기구

grill ⑧ 석쇠에 굽다

nearby ⑲ 근처의, 가까운 곳의

clearly ⑨ 분명히

문제

fool ⑧ 속이다

unpleasant ⑲ 불쾌한

imitate ⑧ 모방하다, 흉내 내다

encourage ⑧ 격려하다

employee ⑲ 직원

Scents can have a powerful effect on our memory. For this reason, some companies use specific scents to _____. Singapore Airlines is one example. They used six kinds of flowers that are native to Singapore to create a signature scent. The scent is used on flight attendant uniforms and in various places on the plane. This makes passengers think of the scent as part of the Singapore Airlines brand image. Another example is Burger King. It uses its vents to spread the smell of grilling burgers. This makes people nearby feel hungry and think of the restaurant. Clearly, companies have learned the power of scents!

1 글의 빈칸에 들어갈 말로 가장 알맞은 것은?

① fool their customers
② hide unpleasant smells
③ imitate other companies
④ encourage their employees
⑤ stay in the minds of customers

서술형

2 다음 회사들은 어떤 방식으로 향기를 이용하고 있는지 우리말로 쓰시오.

(1) Singapore Airlines: _____

(2) Burger King: _____

PSYCHOLOGY

02 ★☆☆
119 words

✎ VOCABULARY

experience 몡 경험 툉 경험하다
everyday 휑 일상적인
object 몡 물건, 물체
take a look at ~을 보다
bowling 몡 볼링
probably 휘 아마
shocked 휑 충격을 받은, 얼떨떨한
survive 툉 생존하다, 살아남다
recognize 툉 알아보다
useful 휑 유용한
sneak up ~에게 몰래 다가가다
normal 휑 정상적인
function 몡 기능
regularly 휘 정기적으로; *자주
[문제]
vision 몡 *시력; 시야
distinguish A from B A와 B를 구별하다
ancestor 몡 조상, 선조

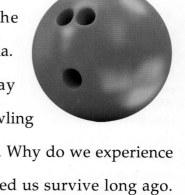

Have you ever seen a face in the clouds? This experience is called *pareidolia. It causes people to see faces in everyday objects. Take a look at the picture of a bowling ball. You can probably see a shocked face. Why do we experience pareidolia? One reason is because it helped us survive long ago. Being able to recognize faces in the dark or hidden in the jungle was a useful skill. It prevented our enemies from sneaking up on us. Also, it is a normal function of the brain. Our brain regularly tries to put parts together to form a full image. This is why we see the three holes of the bowling ball as a shocked face!

*pareidolia 변상증

1 글의 주제로 가장 알맞은 것은?

① why vision is important for survival
② how to distinguish real things from fake ones
③ why people often see faces hidden in objects
④ how our ancestors were able to avoid their enemies
⑤ how people recognize the faces of others

서술형

2 Pareidolia를 경험하는 이유를 뇌 기능 측면에서 우리말로 쓰시오.

_____

✎ VOCABULARY
modern (형) 현대의
product (명) 제품
soap (명) 비누
unfortunately (부) 유감스럽게도
drain (명) 배수관, 하수구
end up 결국 ~하게 되다
absorb (동) 흡수하다
chemical (명) 화학 물질
seafood (명) 해산물
harm (동) 손상시키다, 해를 끼치다
ban (동) 금지하다
[문제]
effort (명) 노력, 수고
reduce (동) 줄이다, 감소시키다
pollution (명) 오염
recycle (동) 재활용하다
influence (명) 영향
negatively (부) 부정적으로

✎ VOCA PLUS
명사 + -ous → 형용사
┌ danger (명) 위험
└ dangerous (형) 위험한
┌ nerve (명) 신경; 긴장, 불안
└ nervous (형) 불안해 하는
┌ fame (명) 명성
└ famous (형) 유명한

Many modern bath products, such as soaps and body washes, contain small pieces of plastic known as "microbeads." These microbeads are usually less than two millimeters wide. Companies use them (people, cleaner, because, feel, they, help). Unfortunately, these small beads have caused big problems. As you wash, microbeads go down the bathroom drain. Eventually, they end up in lakes, rivers, and oceans. There, they absorb dangerous chemicals in the water and are eaten by fish. This means that people who eat seafood could be harmed by microbeads. _____, the United States banned companies from using microbeads in their products in 2015. Many other countries have also done the same. So the next time you're buying bath products, check if they contain microbeads.

1 What is this passage mainly about?

① a new effort to reduce water pollution
② how plastic waste can be safely recycled
③ a company that makes natural bath products
④ why microbeads are used in bath products
⑤ the dangers of small pieces of plastic used in bath products

2 글의 빈칸에 들어갈 말로 가장 알맞은 것은?

① Instead　　　　　　　② In addition
③ For example　　　　　④ For this reason
⑤ On the other hand

서술형

3 글의 ( ) 안에 주어진 단어를 바르게 배열하여 문장을 완성하시오.

_____

서술형

4 글의 내용과 일치하도록 빈칸에 알맞은 말을 | 보기 |에서 골라 쓰시오.

보기		released	absorbed	affected	flow	eat

The influence of microbeads on people		
Cause	• They _____ into rivers and oceans. • Harmful chemicals are _____ by them. • Fish _____ them.
Effect	• People can be negatively _____ by eating seafood.

📚 VOCABULARY

daily ⑱ 매일의

South African ⑱ 남아프리카 공화국의

immediately ⑲ 즉시

fly ⑧ 날다; *비행기를 타고 가다 (fly-flew-flown)

empty ⑱ 빈, 비어 있는

cage ⑲ (짐승의) 우리

aid ⑲ 도움, 조력

zookeeper ⑲ 동물원 사육사

local ⑱ 현지의, 지역의

transport ⑧ 수송하다, 이동 시키다

feed ⑧ 먹이를 주다

volunteer ⑧ 자원하다, 자원 봉사로 하다

escape ⑧ 달아나다, 탈출 하다

organization ⑲ 단체, 기구

supplies ⑲ 보급품

public ⑲ 일반 사람들, 대중

[문제]

rescue ⑲ 구출, 구조

📚 VOCA PLUS

다의어 report

1. ⑲ (뉴스 등의) 보도
   I can't believe the news report.

2. ⑲ 보고서
   Submit your report by this Friday.

3. ⑧ 알리다, 발표하다
   He reported the discovery of a new planet.

4. ⑧ 보고하다, 신고하다
   Report the accident to the police right now!

DAILY NEWS

In 2003, a South African *environmentalist named Lawrence Anthony saw a news report about the Iraq War. Due to the war, animals in the country's biggest zoo were dying. Anthony immediately flew to Baghdad, Iraq, to help. At the Baghdad Zoo, he found many empty cages. Others had dead or dying animals in them. (a) Anthony asked for aid, and both zookeepers and local people agreed to help. (b) They built a **canal to bring water to the surviving zoo animals. (c) Canals are often used to transport goods on boats. (d) And Anthony bought some donkeys to feed to the ***carnivorous animals. (e) Iraqi and US soldiers worked together to help the animals, even though they had been fighting just weeks earlier. They volunteered as guards for the zoo and searched for animals that had escaped. International organizations around the world sent supplies and money to the zoo. Thanks to everyone's efforts, the Baghdad Zoo reopened to the public just six months later.

*environmentalist 환경 운동가 **canal 운하, 수로
***carnivorous 육식성의; 육식 동물의

1 글의 내용과 일치하는 것은?

① 동물원에 있던 대부분의 동물들이 전쟁 속에 살아남았다.
② Anthony는 지역 주민들에게 도움을 요청했으나 거절당했다.
③ Anthony는 동물들을 위해 물과 먹이를 구입했다.
④ 미군과 이라크군은 동물들을 살리기 위해 서로 협력했다.
⑤ Anthony의 구조활동은 국제사회의 관심을 받지 못했다.

2 Which sentence is NOT needed in the passage?

① (a)　　　　② (b)　　　　③ (c)　　　　④ (d)　　　　⑤ (e)

서술형

3 다음 질문에 대한 답을 본문에서 찾아 우리말로 쓰시오.

> Why did Lawrence Anthony buy donkeys?

_____

서술형

4 글의 내용과 일치하도록 빈칸에 알맞은 말을 | 보기 |에서 골라 쓰시오.

| 보기 |　　remaining　　recovered　　joined　　save　　fought

Anthony went to the Baghdad Zoo to _____ animals during the Iraq War.

▼

The _____ animals were near death.

▼

US and Iraqi soldiers _____ the rescue activities.

▼

The Baghdad Zoo _____ because of everyone's efforts.

Talk Talk한
이야기
p. 45

정답 및 해설 p. 17

A   다음 의미에 해당하는 단어를 | 보기 |에서 찾아 쓰시오.

| 보기 | harm   scent   native   memory   volunteer

1 _____ : a pleasant smell

2 _____ : the ability to remember things

3 _____ : originating in a certain place

4 _____ : to offer to do something without being paid for it

5 _____ : to have a bad effect on something or someone

B   다음 밑줄 친 단어와 의미가 반대되는 것을 고르시오.

1 A cell phone is a necessity in <u>modern</u> society.

① new   ② harmful   ③ international   ④ cultural   ⑤ ancient

2 Smoking is <u>banned</u> in this area.

① absorbed   ② allowed   ③ transported   ④ escaped   ⑤ prevented

3 The box is completely <u>empty</u>.

① huge   ② full   ③ light   ④ enough   ⑤ heavy

C   우리말과 같은 뜻이 되도록 빈칸에 들어갈 말을 | 보기 |에서 골라 알맞은 형태로 쓰시오.

| 보기 | end up   sneak up   have an effect on

1 그 소년은 아빠를 놀라게 하려고 그에게 몰래 다가갔다.

The boy _____ on his father to surprise him.

2 그의 가르침은 그의 많은 학생들에게 영향을 끼쳤다.

His teaching _____ many of his students.

3 우리는 비 때문에 결국 집에 머물게 되었다.

We _____ staying home because of the rain.

44

이라크 전쟁은 왜 일어났을까?

앞에 지문을 보니까 궁금한 게 있어. 이라크 전쟁은 왜 일어난 거야?

오래 전부터 이란과 이라크는 정치적, 종교적인 이유로 항상 부딪혀 왔지. 당시 이란은 기독교 성격이 반영된 서구 문화에 적대적이었는데, 미국은 이란의 세력이 커지는 것을 우려해 이라크를 지원하는 쪽이었어. 그때까지만 해도 미국과 이라크는 사이가 나쁘지 않았어.

그럼 미국은 왜 이라크를 공격했어?

여러 가지 이유가 있지만, 가장 대표적인 계기는 9·11 테러(September 11 attacks) 사건이야. 2001년 9월 11일 이슬람 테러리스트들이 민간인이 탄 비행기를 납치해서 뉴욕의 월드 트레이드 센터(the World Trade Center complex)에 추락시켰거든. 이 사고로 무려 3천 명에 가까운 사망자가 발생했지.

이게 9·11 테러 때 사진이야. 월드 트레이드 센터는 원래 쌍둥이 빌딩이었는데, 이 사건 이후로 하나로 줄었어. 지금 이곳엔 피해자들을 기념하는 공원이 있지.

아 너무 끔찍해. 이 사건 이후에 미국은 어떻게 했니?

미국은 당시 이라크의 대통령이었던 사담 후세인(Sadam Hussein)이 테러리스트들을 지원했다고 생각했어. 그래서 2003년 3월 이라크의 수도 바그다드에 보복성 폭격을 가하면서 이라크 전쟁이 시작됐지. 전쟁은 3년 동안 계속되었고, 사담 후세인이 체포되면서 종결되었어. 이 전쟁으로 이라크는 내전과 빈곤이 더 심화되었다고 해. 지금도 이라크 국민들 중에는 미국에 적대적인 감정을 가진 사람들이 많아.

아, 정말 전쟁은 무슨 일이 있어도 용납될 수 없는 거구나. 😖

Section

5

ECONOMY

01

★ ☆ ☆
115 words

✏ **VOCABULARY**

old saying 속담
concept ⑲ 개념
thousands of 수천의
share ⑧ 공유하다
vote for ~에 투표하다
consider ⑧ 고려하다, 검토하다
receive ⑧ 받다
sale ⑲ 판매
win-win ⑲ 모두에게 유리한, 모두가 득을 보는
situation ⑲ 상황
문제
strike ⑧ 때리다, 치다
iron ⑲ 철, 쇠

"_____"

This is an old saying. It means two people can think of twice as many ideas as one person can. Nowadays, companies use this concept with thousands of people. It's called crowdsourcing. A toy company called LEGO is a good example. They have a special website called LEGO Ideas. Anyone can share ideas for new products on this site. If 10,000 people vote for an idea, LEGO will consider it. If they choose it, it will become a real toy. The person who created the product receives a little money from each sale. And, of course, LEGO gets thousands of free ideas for new toys. It's a win-win situation!

1 글의 빈칸에 들어갈 속담으로 가장 알맞은 것은?

① Every dog has his day.
② Practice makes perfect.
③ Strike while the iron is hot.
④ Two heads are better than one.
⑤ Actions speak louder than words.

서술형

2 LEGO는 크라우드소싱을 어떻게 활용하고 있는지 우리말로 간단히 쓰시오. (2가지)

(1) _____

(2) _____

02

★ ☆ ☆
129 words

✎ VOCABULARY

across (전) ~에 걸쳐; 가로질러

turn off ~을 끄다

light (명) 빛; *전등

save (동) 절약하다

billions of 수십억의

migrate (동) (동물이 계절에 따라) 이동하다

follow (동) 따라가다

confuse (동) 혼란시키다

get lost 길을 잃다

crash into ~와 충돌하다

millions of 수백만의

campaign (명) 캠페인, (사회) 운동

encourage (동) 권장하다, 장려하다

unnecessary (형) 불필요한

security (명) 보안, 치안

purpose (명) 목적

cover (동) 가리다, 씌우다

Every spring and fall, cities across America turn their lights off at night. Do they do it just to save energy? No, they do not. There's another reason. During these times, billions of birds migrate across the country. They often fly at night and find their way by following the stars. However, bright lights confuse them. Some get lost, while others crash into the windows of buildings. Millions of birds die (A) this way every year. Lights Out campaigns are designed to help these birds. People and companies are encouraged to turn off all unnecessary lights from 11:00 p.m. to 6:00 a.m. If lights are used for security purposes, they can be covered to make them less bright. Going dark (B) this way not only protects birds but also saves energy.

1 글을 읽고 알 수 있는 내용으로 알맞지 <u>않은</u> 것은?

① 철새들의 이동 시기　　② 철새들의 이동 방법

③ 캠페인의 목적　　④ 캠페인 동안 절약되는 전기의 양

⑤ 전등을 끄는 시간

> 서술형

2 글의 밑줄 친 (A)와 (B)가 각각 의미하는 것을 우리말로 쓰시오.

(A) _____

(B) _____

VOCABULARY

fictional (형) 허구적인, 소설의
detective (명) 탐정
detail (명) 세부 사항
reach (동) ~에 이르다, 닿다
conclusion (명) 결론
case (명) 경우; *사건
Greek (명) 그리스어
suspect (명) 용의자
athlete (명) (운동)선수; *육상
선수
poorly (부) 좋지 못하게, 형편
없이
crime (명) 범죄
clue (명) 단서, 증거
scratch (동) 긁다 *(명) 긁힌
자국
dirt (명) 먼지; *흙
notice (동) 주목하다; 알아채다
slow down (속도를) 늦추다
pay attention to ~에 관심을
기울이다
문제
hard-working (형) 근면한

VOCA PLUS

다의어 subject

1. (명) 주제, 화제
   Climate change is the
   subject of the essay.

2. (명) 학과, 과목
   My favorite subject is
   science.

3. (명) 연구 대상, 피실험자
   Each test subject was
   given five questions.

Sherlock Holmes, a fictional detective, is famous for solving difficult problems. You can be like Sherlock Holmes if you use one important skill: _____. ⓐ He used small details to reach conclusions. For example, Holmes once solved a case of stolen Greek test questions. There were three suspects. The first ⓑ one was an athlete and an excellent student. The second one was smart but lazy. The third one worked hard but did poorly in ⓒ the subject. At the scene of the crime, Holmes discovered two clues: scratches and dirt. Based on ⓓ these, he realized that the thief was the athlete. Athletes wear spiked shoes. The *spikes caused the scratches, and the dirt fell out from between ⓔ them! Holmes solved the case by noticing small things! So slow down and pay attention to the world around you. If you do, you'll notice little but important things, just like Sherlock Holmes.

*spike 스파이크(미끄러지지 않도록 신발 밑창에 박은 뾰족한 못이나 징)

1 What is the best choice for the blank?

① listening   ② patience

③ innovation   ④ observation

⑤ imagination

2 글의 밑줄 친 ⓐ~ⓔ가 가리키는 것으로 옳지 <u>않은</u> 것은?

① ⓐ Sherlock Holmes   ② ⓑ suspect

③ ⓒ Greek   ④ ⓓ clues

⑤ ⓔ shoes

서술형

3 다음 영영 뜻풀이에 해당하는 단어를 본문에서 찾아 쓰시오.

> a specific ability or kind of ability

_____

서술형

4 글의 내용과 일치하도록 빈칸에 알맞은 말을 | 보기 |에서 골라 쓰시오.

| 보기 | scratches   thief   spikes   lazy   athlete   poor

Who stole the greek test questions?	
The suspects	an excellent student who is a(n) _____
	a smart but _____ student
	a hard-working student who is _____ at the subject
Small details	_____ and dirt at the crime scene
Conclusion	Sherlock Holmes discovered the _____ was the athlete.

✎ VOCABULARY

alone (부) 홀로 *(형) 오로지 ~만

invention (명) 발명(품)

originally (부) 원래

pickled (형) (식초에) 절인

similar to ~와 비슷한

soy sauce 간장

thin (형) 얇은; *묽은

trader (명) 상인

introduce (동) 소개하다; *도입하다

merchant (명) 상인

bring ~ back ~을 가지고 돌아가다

local (형) 지역의, 현지의

including (전) ~을 포함하여

mushroom (명) 버섯

oyster (명) 굴

anchovy (명) 멸치

walnut (명) 호두

recipe (명) 조리법

recognize (동) 알다, 알아보다

✎ VOCA PLUS

다의어 adapt

1. (동) (환경에) 적응하다
   The animals have <u>adapted</u> to the weather changes.

2. (동) (새로운 용도·상황에) 맞추다, 조정하다
   This device has been <u>adapted</u> for elderly people.

3. (연극·영화로) 각색하다
   The writer <u>adapted</u> the stories for the movies.

Ketchup has become one of the most popular sauces in the world. In the US alone, millions of tons of ketchup are sold every year. Ketchup, however, is not an American invention. The first ketchup was made in Vietnam and originally contained pickled fish. (A) <u>It</u> looked similar to soy sauce because it was dark and thin. (①) It is believed that Vietnamese traders introduced the sauce to China. (②) There, it was called "keh-jup," which means "fish sauce." (③) Later, in the 18th century, British merchants brought it back to Europe. (④) They adapted the sauce to their taste by adding local foods, including mushrooms, oysters, anchovies, and walnuts. (⑤) But in 1812, an American scientist added tomatoes to ketchup. Food companies added sugar and *vinegar to (B) <u>his</u> recipe. Finally, the sauce became the ketchup we recognize today.

*vinegar 식초

1   글을 읽고 대답할 수 있는 질문이 <u>아닌</u> 것은?

① What did the earliest ketchup contain?
② Where did the name of ketchup come from?
③ How did the earliest ketchup spread to Europe?
④ Who put tomatoes in the ketchup for the first time?
⑤ How many ingredients did Europeans add to ketchup?

2   Where would the following sentence best fit in the passage?

> At this point, it still wasn't similar to modern ketchup.

    ①   ②   ③   ④   ⑤

서술형

3   글의 밑줄 친 (A)와 (B)가 가리키는 것을 본문에서 찾아 영어로 쓰시오. (각 3단어)

(A) _____

(B) _____

서술형

4   글의 내용과 일치하도록 빈칸에 알맞은 말을 본문에서 찾아 쓰시오.

The first ketchup contained _____ fish, and it was dark and _____.

▼

The British merchants added _____ foods to the sauce.

▼

_____ were added to ketchup by an American _____.

▼

Modern ketchup is made with tomatoes, sugar, and _____.

Talk Talk한
이야기
....
p. 55

Section ❺   53

REVIEW TEST

정답 및 해설 p. 21

A 다음 의미에 해당하는 단어를 | 보기 |에서 찾아 쓰시오.

| 보기 | detail   share   local   trader   encourage

1 _____ : someone who buys and sells things

2 _____ : one of many small facts about something

3 _____ : relating to the specific area that someone lives in

4 _____ : to suggest that someone does something

5 _____ : to have something with others or tell them your thoughts

B 다음 밑줄 친 단어와 의미가 반대되는 것을 고르시오.

1 I <u>reached</u> her house last night.

① left ② adapted ③ recognized ④ brought ⑤ rented

2 We should <u>save</u> energy for the future.

① produce ② waste ③ notice ④ provide ⑤ introduce

3 This soup is very <u>thin</u>.

① bitter ② salty ③ thick ④ delicious ⑤ fatty

C 우리말과 같은 뜻이 되도록 빈칸에 들어갈 말을 | 보기 |에서 골라 알맞은 형태로 쓰시오.

| 보기 | turn off   crash into   vote for

1 선거에서 누구한테 투표할 거니?

Who will you _____ in the election?

2 가스 불 끄는 것을 잊지 마라.

Don't forget to _____ the gas.

3 그의 트럭은 버스와 충돌했다.

His truck _____ the bus.

케첩이 약으로 쓰였다고?

옛날에 케첩이 약으로 쓰였단 사실을 알고 있어?

달고 상큼한 케첩이 약으로 쓰였다고? 😮

1834년 미국 의사인 존 쿠크 버넷(John Cooke Bennet)은 케첩의 주재료인 토마토가 설사, 소화불량, 황달과 같은 질병을 치료할 수 있다는 것을 알고, 최초로 케첩을 약으로 제안했어. 그 약의 이름은 "케첩 필(ketchup pill)"이야!

당시 인기는 정말 폭발적이었어. 그 후로 약 20년 동안 많은 약국 회사들이 버넷의 케첩 필을 모방해서 약을 팔았다고 해. 오늘날 우리가 먹는 달달한 케첩과 성분은 조금 다르겠지만 토마토가 그만큼 건강에 좋다는 거겠지?

우와 정말 신기해. 케첩이 약으로 쓰일 정도로 토마토는 건강에 좋은 채소구나! 😎 토마토가 가지고 있는 효능에 대해 구체적으로 알려 줄래?

좋아! 토마토는 라이코펜이라는 핵심 성분을 가지고 있어. 이 성분은 토마토의 붉은 색소를 내는 역할을 하기도 해.
라이코펜은 노화 방지와 항암 효과를 주는 강력한 항산화 기능을 가지고 있어. 이 기능은 무려 비타민 E의 100배나 된대! 암세포로 변할 수 있는 돌연변이 세포의 생성을 막아주고 고혈압을 억제하는 데 도움을 줘.
이외에도 토마토에는 무기질과 비타민이 풍부하고 항암, 피부 미용 등 다양한 효능을 지녀서 세계 10대 슈퍼 푸드 중 하나로 잘 알려져 있지~

토마토를 더 건강하게 먹는 꿀팁이 있어. 토마토를 가열하면 라이코펜 흡수율이 두 배로 높아져.
토마토를 불에 볶아서 섭취하면 몸에 더욱 좋을 거야!

이렇게 말이야?

Section

6

ORIGIN
01
★ ☆ ☆
118 words

VOCABULARY
invent ⑧ 발명하다
straw ⑲ 빨대
improve ⑧ 개선하다
according to ∼에 따르면
historian ⑲ 역사가
ancient ⑱ 고대의
Egyptian ⑲ 이집트인
avoid ⑧ 피하다
material ⑲ 물질
float ⑧ (물 위에) 뜨다
royalty ⑲ 왕족
share ⑧ 함께 쓰다, 공유하다
reed ⑲ 갈대
wrap ⑧ (포장지로) 싸다
glue ⑲ 접착제 *⑧ (접착제로)
붙이다
cover ⑧ 덮다; *바르다

It is often said that Marvin Stone invented the drinking straw, but that's not true. He only improved it. (a) According to historians, ancient Egyptians used straws to drink beer. (b) They did so to avoid drinking material floating in the beer. (c) For hundreds of years, beer has been one of the most popular drinks in the world. (d) *Babylonian royalty also drank beer this way, although they used straws made of gold! (e) And according to a 6,000-year-old text, ancient **Sumerians sometimes shared drinks by using straws made of reed. Much later, in 1888, Marvin Stone invented the first paper straw. He wrapped pieces of paper around a pencil and then glued them together. He later improved his design by covering the paper in wax so it wouldn't get wet. This became the straw we use today.

*Babylonian 바빌로니아의   **Sumerian 수메르 사람

1 문장 (a)~(e) 중 글의 흐름과 관계가 <u>없는</u> 것은?

① (a)   ② (b)   ③ (c)   ④ (d)   ⑤ (e)

서술형

2 사람들이 각각 빨대의 주재료로 사용한 것을 본문에서 찾아 영어로 쓰시오. (각 1단어)

(1) Babylonian royalty: _____

(2) ancient Sumerians: _____

(3) Marvin Stone: _____

CULTURE

02 ★ ☆ ☆
118 words

VOCABULARY

march 동 행진하다

joyful 형 즐거운

funeral 명 장례식

celebrate 동 기념하다,
축하하다

good 형 좋은 *타당한

slave 명 노예

free 형 자유로운, 자유의
동 자유롭게 하다, 해방하다

express 동 표현하다

soul 명 영혼

homeland 명 고국, 모국

death 명 죽음

though 접 비록 ~이지만

disappear 동 사라지다

문제

cheerful 형 발랄한, 쾌활한

In New Orleans, you can see marching jazz bands playing joyful music during funerals. This might seem strange, but African Americans in New Orleans often celebrate at funerals. There is a good reason for this. (①) When Africans were brought to New Orleans hundreds of years ago, they worked as slaves and had hard lives. (②) In their free time, they used music to express their feelings. (③) They believed that when they died, their souls would fly back to their homeland. (④) In other words, death would free them from their hard lives. (⑤) Though *slavery has disappeared from New Orleans, people still enjoy music at funerals, just like in the past.

*slavery 노예 제도

1 글의 흐름으로 보아 주어진 문장이 들어갈 위치로 가장 적절한 곳은?

> That's why people celebrate with cheerful jazz music at funerals.

① ② ③ ④ ⑤

서술형

2 과거 뉴올리언스의 노예들은 죽으면 영혼이 어떻게 된다고 믿었는지 우리말로 쓰시오.

_____

VOCABULARY

major (형) 주요한
source (명) 원천, 근원
be scared of ~을 무서워
하다
poisonous (형) 독이 있는
in addition 게다가
raw (형) 날것의, 익히지 않은
serious (형) 심각한
despite (전) ~에도 불구하고
soldier (명) 군인, 병사
watch over ~을 지키다,
감시하다
precious (형) 귀중한, 값비싼
across (전) 가로질러; *~ 전체
에 걸쳐
nickname (명) 별명
(문제)
properly (부) 적절히, 제대로
royal (형) 왕실의, 왕족의
throughout (전) ~의 도처에

VOCA PLUS

신체 부위 + -ache
→ ~통, 병

⌐ stomach (명) 위, 복부
└ stomachache (명) 복통
⌐ head (명) 머리
└ headache (명) 두통
⌐ tooth (명) 치아
└ toothache (명) 치통
⌐ ear (명) 귀
└ earache (명) 이통, 귓병
⌐ back (명) 허리, 등
└ backache (명) 요통

Potatoes are one of the world's major sources of food. But in the 16th century, Europeans did not like them. (a) Some Europeans called the potato the devil's plant because it grows underground. (b) Other people were scared of the plant's poisonous flowers. (c) Potatoes seemed to grow well in hot weather. (d) In addition, people ate raw potatoes because they did not know how to cook them. (e) This caused them to have serious stomachaches. Despite these problems, Friedrich II, King of *Prussia, thought potatoes could be a big help to his hungry people. So the king told his soldiers to plant potatoes in his garden. Then he ordered the soldiers to watch over them. This made people think the potatoes were precious. So people started growing potatoes themselves and even sold them in markets. Soon, potatoes became popular across Europe. That's how Friedrich II got his nickname, the Potato King.

*Prussia 프로이센(독일 북부의 주이자 옛 왕국)

1 What is the best title for the passage?

① Why Europeans Dislike Potatoes
② How Potatoes Became the Food of the Devil
③ How to Grow Potatoes Properly
④ Why Royal Families Protected Their Potatoes
⑤ How Potatoes Became Common Throughout Europe

2 유럽의 감자에 대한 설명 중 글의 내용과 일치하지 <u>않는</u> 것은?

① 감자는 땅속에서 자라므로 악마의 식물이라고 불렸다.
② 감자의 꽃은 독성을 띠고 있다.
③ 감자를 생으로 먹으면 배탈이 날 수 있다.
④ Friedrich 2세는 감자를 즐겨 먹었다.
⑤ Friedrich 2세 덕분에 감자가 유럽에서 인기를 얻었다.

3 문장 (a)~(e) 중 글의 흐름과 관계가 <u>없는</u> 것은?

① (a) ② (b) ③ (c) ④ (d) ⑤ (e)

서술형

4 사람들이 감자를 먹게 하기 위해 Friedrich 2세가 병사들에게 시킨 일을 우리말로 쓰시오. (2가지)

(1) _____

(2) _____

VOCABULARY

branch 명 나뭇가지
root 명 뿌리
legend 명 전설
create 동 창조하다
proud 형 자랑스러워하는;
*거만한
upset 형 속상한, 화가 난
plant 동 (식물을) 심다
upside down 거꾸로, 뒤집혀
envy 동 부러워하다;
*질투하다
height 명 높이, 키
pull ~ up ~을 뽑다, 빼다
punish 동 처벌하다, 벌주다
문제
show off ~을 자랑하다

VOCA PLUS

re- + 동사 → 다시 ~하다
┌ plant 동 심다
└ replant 동 다시 심다
┌ fill 동 채우다
└ refill 동 다시 채우다
┌ write 동 쓰다
└ rewrite 동 다시[고쳐] 쓰다
┌ place 동 두다, 배치하다
└ replace 동 교체[대체]하다

The baobab tree is a strange-looking tree found in Africa and Australia. It doesn't have leaves until it is nine years old. Without leaves, the tree's branches ⓐ look like roots. So the baobab tree ⓑ is known by the nickname "upside-down tree." There are even legends about this strange-looking tree. One legend says God created the baobab as the strongest tree in the world. Because the baobab knew that, it was very proud. It tried to show everyone ⓒ how great was it by moving all around. This made God upset, so God took the baobab out of the ground and planted it upside down.

Another legend says the baobab was the first tree in the world. After the baobab was created, the *palm tree, the **flame tree, and the ***fig tree were created. The other trees each had something the baobab didn't have, so the baobab tree envied them. The baobab wanted to have the palm tree's height, the flame tree's beautiful flowers, and the fig tree's fruit, so it asked God to have all of them. God became angry, ⓓ pulled it up, and then replanted it upside down ⓔ to punish it.

*palm tree 종려나무　**flame tree 불꽃나무　***fig tree 무화과나무

62

1 바오밥 나무에 대한 두 전설이 공통적으로 이야기하고 있는 것은?

① 바오밥 나무가 잎이 없는 이유
② 바오밥 나무가 흔하지 않은 이유
③ 바오밥 나무가 키가 크고 튼튼한 이유
④ 바오밥 나무가 다른 나무들을 시기한 이유
⑤ 바오밥 나무가 거꾸로 심은 것처럼 보이는 이유

2 Which is NOT grammatically correct among ⓐ~ⓔ?

① ⓐ   ② ⓑ   ③ ⓒ   ④ ⓓ   ⑤ ⓔ

서술형

3 바오밥 나무가 upside-down tree라고 알려진 이유를 우리말로 쓰시오.

_____

서술형

4 글의 내용과 일치하도록 빈칸에 알맞은 말을 |보기|에서 골라 쓰시오.

|보기|	first replanted power strongest flowers planted
The first legend	• The baobab was the _____ tree on Earth. • It went around everywhere to show off its _____. • So God angrily _____ it upside down.
The second legend	• The baobab was the world's _____ tree. • It asked God for the height of the palm tree, the _____ of the flame tree, and the fruit of the fig tree. • God got angry and _____ it upside down.

Talk Talk한
이야기
p. 65

A 다음 의미에 해당하는 단어를 | 보기 |에서 찾아 쓰시오.

| 보기 |　　　legend　　　float　　　punish　　　proud　　　funeral

1 _____: to stay on top of a liquid without sinking

2 _____: an old story about people or events

3 _____: a ceremony that is held after someone dies

4 _____: feeling like you are better or more important than others

5 _____: to make someone suffer because they did something wrong

B 다음 밑줄 친 단어와 의미가 반대되는 것을 고르시오.

1 Children usually don't like raw vegetables.
① rare　　　② cool　　　③ cooked　　　④ fresh　　　⑤ healthy

2 We were joyful when we heard the news.
① sad　　　② excited　　　③ jealous　　　④ pleased　　　⑤ nervous

3 His coat was wet when he came inside.
① dry　　　② dirty　　　③ heavy　　　④ fancy　　　⑤ expensive

C 우리말과 같은 뜻이 되도록 빈칸에 들어갈 말을 | 보기 |에서 골라 알맞은 형태로 쓰시오.

| 보기 |　　　pull up　　　watch over　　　be scared of

1 나의 개는 혼자서 자는 것을 무서워한다.
My dog _____ sleeping alone.

2 이것들이 내가 오늘 뽑은 당근들이야.
These are the carrots that I _____ today.

3 그 소년은 양떼를 지키고 있었다.
The boy was _____ a flock of sheep.

아낌없이 주는 바오밥 나무

날 생명의 나무라 불러 줘

프랑스의 소설가 생텍쥐페리(Saint-Exupéry)의 동화 '어린 왕자(The Little Prince)'에서 바오밥 나무는 무시무시한 크기로 작은 별을 휘감아 파괴하는 골칫거리로 여겨졌어요. 하지만 아프리카 주민들은 바오밥 나무를 '생명의 나무'라고 부른답니다. 바오밥 나무는 대체로 천 년 이상을 살 수 있어요! 또 바오밥 나무는 생태계에서 매우 중요한 역할을 하지요. 줄기에 수분을 가득 머금고 있어서 다양한 생물들에게 풍부한 영양분을 제공하고, 그 큰 몸집으로 아늑한 쉼터와 서식처가 되어 주지요.

바오밥 나무의 다양한 쓰임

바오밥 나무의 잎은 햇빛에 말려 나물로 먹을 수 있고 가축의 먹이도 된답니다. 또한 감기나 다양한 질병을 치료하는 약으로 쓰이기도 합니다.

바오밥 꽃은 주로 밤에 피고 강한 향기와 달콤한 꿀을 갖고 있어요. 그래서 야행성인 박쥐가 꿀을 먹고 수분시키는 역할을 해요.

바오밥 열매의 가루를 물에 섞으면 주스가 됩니다. 설탕이나 소금을 추가로 넣어 먹기도 해요.

과거에 아프리카 주민들은 바오밥 나무를 건물처럼 이용하기도 했습니다. 창고, 식당, 우체국, 화장실, 감옥까지! 엄청 큰 크기를 자랑하는 줄기 안을 깊숙이 파내서 공간을 만들었다고 해요.

www.nebooks.co.kr

Section

7

✎ VOCABULARY

put on ~을 입다, 신다
tie ⑧ (매듭을) 묶다, 매다
shoelace ⑲ 신발 끈
tightly ⑨ 단단히, 꽉
untied ⑲ 묶이지 않은, 풀린
happen ⑧ 일어나다, 생기다
mystery ⑲ 미스터리, 난제
high-speed ⑲ 고속의
film ⑧ 촬영하다, 찍다
untie ⑧ 매듭을 풀다
force ⑲ 힘
impact ⑲ 영향; *충돌, 충격
knot ⑲ 매듭
stretch ⑧ 늘어나다, 신축성이
있다
loosen ⑧ 느슨해지다, 풀리다
shake ⑧ 흔들리다
pull on ~을 잡아당기다

First you put on your shoes. Then you tie your shoelaces tightly. One hour later, however, they are untied. Why does this happen? It was a mystery until recently. Researchers used a high-speed camera to film the shoelaces of a person running on a *treadmill. For a long time, the shoelaces stayed tightly tied. And then they suddenly untied! According to the researchers, there are two reasons for this. (a) The first reason is the force of a person's foot hitting the ground when they walk. (b) This impact causes the knots in the shoelaces to stretch and loosen. (c) There are a few ways to prevent the shoelaces from untying. (d) The second reason is the shaking of the ends of the shoelaces. (e) As they shake, they pull on the knot, slowly untying it.

*treadmill 러닝머신

1 문장 (a)~(e) 중 글의 흐름과 관계가 <u>없는</u> 것은?

① (a)　　② (b)　　③ (c)　　④ (d)　　⑤ (e)

서술형

2 꽉 묶은 신발 끈이 풀리는 이유를 본문에서 찾아 우리말로 쓰시오. (2가지)

(1) _____

(2) _____

SPACE

02

★ ☆ ☆

106 words

VOCABULARY

planet 몡 행성
Jupiter 몡 목성
moon 몡 달; *위성
interestingly 틘 흥미롭게도
volcano 몡 화산
surface 몡 표면
opposite 혱 정반대의,
상반하는
rock 몡 암석
volcanic 혱 화산의
eruption 몡 (화산의) 폭발,
분화
process 몡 과정
hundreds of 수백의

The planet Jupiter has almost one hundred moons. Interestingly, one of these moons has lots of volcanoes on its surface! It is called Io, and it's Jupiter's third largest moon. It *orbits the planet closer than the two larger moons. As a result, the **gravitational forces of Jupiter and the other moons pull on Io in opposite directions. This creates heat inside Io and melts the rock inside it. When the rock melts, it causes volcanic eruptions. Over time, this process has created more and more volcanoes on Io. In fact, there are hundreds of volcanoes now. And some of them are bigger than Mount Everest!

*orbit 궤도를 돌다   **gravitational 중력의

1 Io에 대한 설명 중 글의 내용과 일치하지 <u>않는</u> 것은?

① Io는 목성의 위성 중 세 번째로 크다.
② Io는 다른 더 큰 위성들보다 목성에 더 가깝다.
③ Io의 화산 활동은 목성과 위성들의 중력에 의한 것이다.
④ Io의 화산 수는 점점 감소하고 있다.
⑤ Io의 화산 중 일부는 에베레스트 산보다 더 크다.

서술형

2 다음 질문에 대한 답을 본문에서 찾아 영어로 쓰시오. (9단어)

What pulls on Io in opposite directions?

Callisto

Ganymede

Io

📖 **VOCABULARY**

hurt (형) 상처를 입은, 다친
(동) 다치게 하다, 아프게 하다
situation (명) 상황
burn (명) 화상, 덴 상처
run (동) 달리다; *(액체를) 흐르게
하다
cloth (명) 천, 옷감
protect (동) 보호하다, 막다
further (형) 더 이상의, 추가의
damage (명) 손상, 피해
bite (명) 물기, 무는 행위
additional (형) 추가의
slow down (속도를) 늦추다
spread (명) 확산
venom (명) (뱀·곤충의) 독
panic (명) 공황 상태
heart rate 심박동수
speed up 속도를 내다
sting (명) 쏘인 상처 (동) 쏘다,
찌르다 (sting-stung-stung)
remove (동) 제거하다
apply (동) (물건을) 대다
pain (명) 고통
문제
substance (명) 물질

🔖 **VOCA PLUS**

명사 + -ful → 형용사
- help (명) 도움
- helpful (형) 도움이 되는
- cheer (명) 환호; 활기
- cheerful (형) 발랄한, 쾌활한
- care (명) 돌봄; 조심, 주의
- careful (형) 조심하는, 주의
깊은

Knowing what to do when someone gets hurt can be very helpful. Here are some tips for possible situations:

Hot water burns: If the burn is serious, you should take the person to the hospital. If it is small, run cold water over the burn and cover it with a clean cloth. This protects it from the air so it hurts less. Do not use any oils or creams on it, as they can cause further damage to the skin.

Snake bites: First, get the person away from the snake to avoid additional bites. After that, they should keep their body very still. This will slow down the spread of the venom. Make sure they stay calm. Panic can cause their heart rate to increase. It can speed up the spread of the venom as well.

Bee stings: If someone is stung by a bee, you should remove the *stinger immediately. Next, wash the **affected area with soap and water, and then apply ice to reduce the ***swelling and pain. If the person has difficulty breathing, take them to a doctor right away.

*stinger (동물의) 침   **affected area 상처 부위   ***swelling (살갗의) 부기

1 다음 응급조치 요령은 어떤 상황에 필요한 것인지 | 보기 |에서 골라 쓰시오.

	보기		bee stings	snake bites	hot water burns

(1) 환자의 움직임을 최소화하여 독이 퍼지지 않게 한다. _____

(2) 침을 제거하고 상처 부위를 깨끗이 씻어 낸다. _____

(3) 상처 부위를 찬물로 식힌 후 깨끗한 천으로 감싼다. _____

2 화상 부위에 크림이나 오일을 바르면 안 되는 이유는?

① 세균에 감염될 수 있으므로
② 병원 치료 시 방해가 되므로
③ 공기와의 접촉이 차단되므로
④ 화상 부위의 열이 쉽게 식지 않으므로
⑤ 피부에 추가적인 손상이 있을 수 있으므로

서술형

3 다음 영영 뜻풀이에 해당하는 단어를 본문에서 찾아 쓰시오.

> to put a substance onto a surface

_____

서술형

4 다음 질문에 대한 답을 본문에서 찾아 우리말로 쓰시오.

> Why should ice be put on a bee sting?

_____

Talk Talk한 이야기 p. 75

VOCABULARY

stand for ~을 상징하다,
의미하다
miss out ~을 놓치다
refer to ~을 나타내다
anxiety 몡 불안, 걱정
social 혱 사회의; *사교적인
compare 됭 비교하다
peer 몡 또래
in contrast 그에 반해서
pleasure 몡 기쁨, 즐거움
activity 몡 활동
focus on ~에 집중하다
be satisfied with ~에
만족하다
relationship 몡 관계
efficiently 분 효율적으로
suffer from ~으로 고통받다
attend 됭 참석하다
involve 됭 포함하다, 수반하다
device 몡 (기계) 장치, 기기
문제
gathering 몡 모임

VOCA PLUS

다의어 join

1. 가입하다
   I joined a literary club
   because I like writing.

2. 연결하다, 잇다
   Join the two pieces of
   paper with this piece of
   tape.

3. (행위 등에) 함께 하다
   Will you join us for
   some tea?

FOMO stands for the "fear of missing out." It refers to the anxiety of feeling like you're missing out on a social event. This causes people with FOMO to constantly check their phones. They also compare their own lives to the ones of their peers on social media.

In contrast, JOMO stands for the "joy of missing out." It refers to the pleasure of spending time alone instead of joining social activities. People with JOMO focus on themselves, so they are more satisfied with their lives. Also, they tend to have relationships only with people they actually like. As a result, they use their time and energy more efficiently.

Do you suffer from FOMO? JOMO might be the answer. You can start by saying "no." You don't need to attend every social event. You can also try a digital *detox. This involves taking a break from your devices. If you're successful, you'll be able to focus more on your life.

*detox(ification) 해독, 디톡스

1 글의 요지로 가장 알맞은 것은?

① FOMO는 최신 정보를 얻는 데 도움이 된다.
② FOMO는 소셜 미디어 사용으로 인한 부작용이다.
③ JOMO는 시간을 효율적으로 사용하는 효과가 있다.
④ JOMO는 FOMO를 극복하기 위한 해결책이다.
⑤ FOMO와 JOMO는 일상생활에 큰 영향을 미친다.

2 다음 중 FOMO를 겪고 있는 사람끼리 짝지어진 것은?

> 영민: 전화기가 손에 없으면 너무 불안해.
> 희영: 나는 가족들과 보내는 시간이 제일 소중해.
> 서진: 파티에 초대받았는데 안 갈래. 집에서 책보는 게 더 좋아.
> 민호: 친구가 새로 산 운동화를 SNS에 올렸는데 나도 사고 싶어.

① 희영, 민호　　　　　　　　② 서진, 민호
③ 영민, 민호　　　　　　　　④ 영민, 서진
⑤ 영민, 희영

서술형

3 글의 밑줄 친 a digital detox가 의미하는 것을 우리말로 간단히 쓰시오.

_____

서술형

4 글의 내용과 일치하도록 빈칸에 알맞은 말을 본문에서 찾아 쓰시오.

	Meaning	**Behavior**
FOMO	worried about _____ _____ on something	often _____ your phone
JOMO	happy about not joining _____ gatherings	use your _____ and _____ for yourself

정답 및 해설 p. 29

A 다음 의미에 해당하는 단어를 | 보기 |에서 찾아 쓰시오.

| 보기 |　　planet　　shake　　protect　　mystery　　additional

1 _____ : extra or more than expected

2 _____ : something that is unknown or difficult to explain

3 _____ : to move from side to side or up and down

4 _____ : to keep someone or something from harm

5 _____ : a large, round object that moves around a star in space

B 다음 밑줄 친 단어와 의미가 비슷한 것을 고르시오.

1 You have to <u>reduce</u> your speed in the snow.

　① spread　　② happen　　③ disappear　　④ increase　　⑤ decrease

2 The metal was pulled by a strong magnetic <u>force</u>.

　① device　　② power　　③ pain　　④ purpose　　⑤ result

3 My shoelace came <u>untied</u>.

　① tight　　② fixed　　③ active　　④ still　　⑤ loose

C 우리말과 같은 뜻이 되도록 빈칸에 들어갈 말을 | 보기 |에서 골라 알맞은 형태로 쓰시오.

| 보기 |　　　　put on　　　focus on　　　stand for

1 너는 공부에 집중해야 한다.

　You must _____ your studies.

2 그녀는 새 코트를 입었다.

　She _____ her new coat.

3 KTX는 'Korea Train Express'를 의미한다.

　KTX _____ Korea Train Express.

Talk Talk한 이야기

반드시 알아두자, 생명 구조술!

골든타임(Golden time)이라는 말을 들어보았나요? 원래는 방송국에서 청취율이나 시청률이 가장 높은 시간대를 일컫는 말이었지만, 요새는 사고 발생 후 의료적 처치가 이루어져야 하는 최소한의 시간을 의미하며, 골든아워(golden hour)라고도 하지요. 골든타임을 지켜 생명 구조술을 실시하면 응급 상황에 처한 사람들을 살릴 수 있답니다.

숨을 쉬지 않을 때, 심폐소생술 (CPR)

① 환자의 머리를 젖히고, 턱을 들어 올려 기도를 개방합니다.

② 환자의 코를 막고 환자의 입에 본인의 입을 밀착시킨 후, 환자의 가슴이 올라올 정도로 1초 동안 숨을 힘껏 불어 넣습니다. 인공호흡법을 모르면 지속적으로 가슴만 압박합니다.

③ 구조 요원이 도착할 때까지 30회 반복해서 시행합니다. (가슴을 깊게 누르며 분당 100~120번 압박하는 것이 1회)

④ 환자가 호흡을 되찾으면 기도가 막히는 것을 방지하기 위해 몸을 옆으로 눕힙니다.

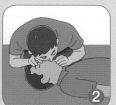

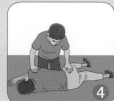

이물질로 기도가 막혔을 때, 하임리히법 (Heimlich Maneuver)

환자가 의식이 있고 말을 할 수 있는 경우에는 기침을 유도합니다. 기침을 해도 이물질이 배출되지 않을 때는 즉시 119로 연락합니다. 환자가 말을 할 수 없는 상황이라면 119에 신고한 후 하임리히법을 실시하고, 환자가 의식이 없는 상태라면 즉시 CPR(심폐소생술)을 실시합니다.

① 환자의 등 뒤에서 양팔로 허리를 감싸도록 합니다.

② 구조자는 왼손으로 주먹을 쥔 후, 환자의 명치와 배꼽 사이에 대고 오른손으로 주먹을 감싸도록 합니다.

③ 빠르게 위로(후상 방향) 힘껏 밀쳐 올립니다.

④ 이물질이 밖으로 나오거나 119 구급대원이 도착할 때까지 위의 과정을 반복합니다.

www.nebooks.co.kr

Section

8

✎ VOCABULARY

taste ⑧ 맛이 ~하다
pick ⑧ 고르다; *(과일 등을) 따다
what if ~? ~라면 어떻게 될까?
refrigerator ⑲ 냉장고
instead of ~ 대신에
soil ⑲ 흙, 땅
oxygen ⑲ 산소
shopper ⑲ 쇼핑객, 고객
save ⑧ 절약하다
transport ⑧ 운송하다
from far away 먼 곳으로부터

Everyone likes fresh vegetables. And they taste best when you pick them yourself. But what if you don't have your own garden? If you live in Berlin, it's not a problem! (a) That's because there is a vegetable garden inside the Metro supermarket. (b) The garden looks like a supermarket refrigerator. (c) Inside it, plants grow in water instead of soil. (d) The soil helps the plants grow. (e) The plants get oxygen and *fertilizer from the water, and they get light from lamps. Shoppers like the garden because they can buy fresh vegetables even in winter. And the supermarket saves money because it doesn't have to transport vegetables from far away. It really is a great idea!

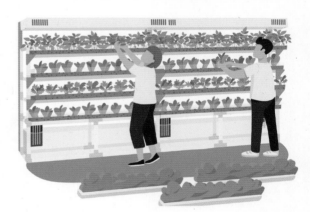

*fertilizer 비료, 거름

---

1 문장 (a)~(e) 중 글의 흐름과 관계가 <u>없는</u> 것은?

① (a)   ② (b)   ③ (c)   ④ (d)   ⑤ (e)

서술형

2 마트에서 직접 채소를 재배하여 판매할 때 고객과 마트의 입장에서 좋은 점을 우리말로 쓰시오.

(1) 고객: _____

(2) 마트: _____

78

VOCABULARY

throughout (전) ~동안 쭉, 내내
cosmetics (명) 화장품
deadly (형) 생명을 앗아갈, 치명적인
lead (명) 납
poisonous (형) 독성이 있는
fashionable (형) 유행하는
pale (형) 창백한
regularly (부) 정기적으로; *자주
side effect 부작용
dizziness (명) 현기증, 어지럼증
ingredient (명) 재료, 성분
juice (명) 즙
period (명) 기간, 시기
regular (형) 정기적인; *잦은
lead to ~으로 이어지다
vision (명) 시력
blindness (명) 실명
문제
achieve (동) 이루다, 성취하다
powder (명) 파우더, 가루

Throughout history, many cultures have used cosmetics. Some cosmetics, however, were dangerous or even deadly! Many cosmetics used to contain lead, which is poisonous. (①) In ancient Greece, it was fashionable for women to have very pale skin. (②) After using it regularly, many women suffered from serious side effects, such as headaches, stomachaches and dizziness. (③) Some even died. (④) Another dangerous ingredient was *belladonna, a poisonous plant. (⑤) European women used the juice from this plant to make their **pupils bigger during ***the Renaissance period. Regular use of belladonna led to poor vision and sometimes blindness. Thankfully, cosmetics are much safer today.

*belladonna 벨라도나(가짓과의 유독성 식물)   **pupil 눈동자, 동공
***the Renaissance 르네상스, 문예 부흥기

1 글의 주제로 가장 알맞은 것은?

① 과거에 사용한 화장품의 위험성
② 화장품이 만들어지는 과정
③ 미백 화장품이 발명된 시기
④ 피부에 좋지 않은 화장품 성분
⑤ 문화에 따른 화장법의 차이

2 글의 흐름으로 보아 주어진 문장이 들어갈 위치로 가장 적절한 곳은?

> To achieve this, they used a face powder that was made from lead, egg whites, and wax.

①   ②   ③   ④   ⑤

VOCABULARY

environmental ⑱ 환경의, 환경과 관련된

activist ⑲ 운동가, 활동가

strategy ⑲ 전략

get one's attention ~의 관심을 얻다

trash ⑲ 쓰레기

produce ⑧ 생산하다, 만들어 내다

be focused 집중하다

seriousness ⑲ 심각성

suit ⑲ 정장; *옷 (한 벌)

plastic bag 비닐봉지

piece ⑲ 부분, 조각

huge ⑱ 큰, 거대한

difference ⑲ 차이

〔문제〕

recycle ⑧ 재활용하다

unique ⑱ 독특한, 특이한

garbage ⑲ 쓰레기

VOCA PLUS

다의어 waste

1. ⑲ 쓰레기
   food waste

2. ⑲ 낭비
   waste of time

3. ⑧ 낭비하다
   She wasted money on clothes.

Robin Greenfield is an environmental activist. One time, he used a special strategy to get people's attention. He wore real trash for a month! He did this to show how much waste people produce every day. Greenfield wasn't always an activist. He used to always be focused on making money. But after reading some books and watching some documentaries, he realized the seriousness of environmental problems. He decided to wear trash because most people don't know how much waste they produce. He made a suit out of plastic bags and then added every piece of trash that he produced for a month. He hoped that people would think about the waste they produce after seeing him. According to Greenfield, it could make a huge difference if people just make small changes.

1 What is the best title for the passage?

① How to Recycle Trash
② The Best Way to Reduce Trash
③ Can We Make Clothes with Trash?
④ An Environmental Activist's Unique Idea
⑤ The History of Environmental Activists

2 Robin Greenfield에 대한 설명 중 글의 내용과 일치하면 T, 그렇지 않으면 F를 쓰시오.

(1) 어린 시절부터 환경에 관심이 많았다. ＿＿＿＿＿

(2) 한 달 동안 자신이 버린 쓰레기로 옷을 만들어 입었다. ＿＿＿＿＿

(3) 사람들이 만드는 작은 변화가 큰 차이를 만들 것이라 믿는다. ＿＿＿＿＿

서술형

3 Robin Greenfield가 환경 운동가가 된 계기를 본문에서 찾아 우리말로 쓰시오.

＿＿＿＿＿＿＿＿＿＿＿＿＿＿＿＿＿＿＿＿＿＿＿＿＿＿＿＿＿＿

서술형

4 글의 내용과 일치하도록 빈칸에 알맞은 말을 | 보기 |에서 골라 쓰시오.

| 보기 |　　special　　realize　　garbage　　catch　　environmental

Robin Greenfield works as a(n) ＿＿＿＿＿＿＿ activist. Once, he put on a suit made of plastic bags to ＿＿＿＿＿＿＿ people's attention. The plastic bags were full of ＿＿＿＿＿＿＿. He did this to make people ＿＿＿＿＿＿＿ how much waste they make.

Talk Talk한
이야기
p. 85

VOCABULARY

weather 명 날씨
forecaster 명 (일기) 예보관
at the same time 동시에
confused 형 혼란스러워
하는, 헷갈리는
name A after B B의 이름을
따서 A의 이름을 짓다
wander 동 헤매다, 떠돌아다
니다
the Pacific 태평양
major 형 주요한, 중대한
several 형 몇몇의
one by one 하나씩, 차례차례
damage 명 손해, 피해
instead 부 대신에
문제
prediction 명 예측
horrible 형 끔찍한

VOCA PLUS

자연재해와 관련된 어휘
typhoon 명 태풍
flood 명 홍수
drought 명 가뭄
earthquake 명 지진
tsunami 명 해일, 쓰나미

Until the late 1800s, typhoons were not given names. Weather forecasters just called each one "a typhoon." When a country had two typhoons at the same time, people got confused. They didn't know which typhoon the forecasters were talking about. So weather forecasters needed to give a name to each typhoon. At first, they named typhoons after real people. Sometimes, they named them after famous people they didn't like. This way, they could say things like, "Ellen is wandering around the Pacific," or "David is becoming weaker and weaker." (a) Today, typhoons are named after people, flowers, animals, and many other things. (b) There are major typhoons every summer. (c) Several countries located in or near the Pacific have made a list of 140 names for typhoons. (d) The names are used one by one. (e) After all of the names are used, the weather forecasters go back to the first name. If a typhoon causes a lot of damage, the name is not used again. They choose a new name instead.

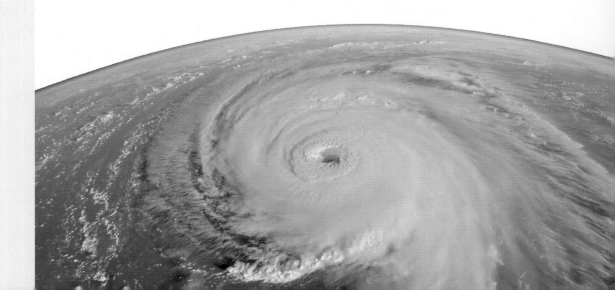

1 글의 제목으로 가장 적절한 것은?

① Different Types of Typhoons
② The History of Naming Typhoons
③ The Difficulty of Weather Prediction
④ The Most Horrible Typhoon in History
⑤ Typhoons Named After Famous People

2 Which sentence is NOT needed in the passage?

① (a)   ② (b)   ③ (c)   ④ (d)   ⑤ (e)

3 글의 내용과 일치하면 T, 그렇지 않으면 F를 쓰시오.

(1) 1800년대 이전에는 태풍의 이름이 따로 없었다.   _____

(2) 태풍 목록에 있는 이름을 다 사용하면 새로운 이름을 만든다.   _____

(3) 피해가 큰 태풍의 이름은 다시 사용하지 않는다.   _____

서술형

4 다음 질문에 대한 답을 본문에서 찾아 우리말로 쓰시오.

> How did weather forecasters originally name typhoons?

_____

정답 및 해설 p. 32

A 다음 의미에 해당하는 단어를 | 보기 |에서 찾아 쓰시오.

| 보기 | major   strategy   transport   wander   oxygen

1 _____ : a plan for achieving a goal

2 _____ : great in size, importance, or extent

3 _____ : to move around without a particular destination

4 _____ : to carry people or things from one place to another

5 _____ : a gas that people and animals need to breathe in order to live

B 다음 밑줄 친 단어와 의미가 비슷한 것을 고르시오.

1 Julie lives alone in a <u>huge</u> house.

① small   ② large   ③ pleasant   ④ safe   ⑤ horrible

2 We must reduce the amount of <u>trash</u> we create.

① energy   ② pollution   ③ dust   ④ leftover   ⑤ waste

3 Peanuts can be <u>deadly</u> for people with allergies.

① rot   ② dead   ③ effective   ④ precious   ⑤ dangerous

C 우리말과 같은 뜻이 되도록 빈칸에 들어갈 말을 | 보기 |에서 골라 알맞은 형태로 쓰시오.

| 보기 | lead to   suffer from   get one's attention

1 그녀는 그들의 주의를 끌기 위해 박수를 쳤다.

She clapped her hands to _____.

2 부정직함은 신뢰의 상실로 이어질 수 있다.

Dishonesty can _____ a loss of trust.

3 많은 사람들이 아직도 굶주림으로 고통받는다.

Many people still _____ hunger.

Talk Talk한 이야기

지구를 지키는 원더우먼들!

나무들의 어머니, 왕가리 무타 마타이 (Wangari Muta Maathai)

왕가리 무타 마타이는 케냐 출신의 환경 운동가이자 여성 인권 운동가예요. 마타이는 사막화를 막기 위해 1977년부터 나무를 심는 운동을 주도했고, 케냐 전국에 무려 4500만여 그루의 나무를 심었어요! 그녀는 1991년에 환경 운동가들의 노벨상으로 불리는 골드만 환경상을, 2004년에는 노벨 평화상을 수상하기도 했죠.

나무 심기에 대한 열정 때문에 그녀에게는 '마마 미티(Mama Miti)'라는 별명이 생겼는데요. '마마 미티'는 스와힐리(Swahili) 말로 '나무 어머니'라는 뜻이에요.

안타깝게도 71세의 나이로 사망했지만 그녀가 죽은 이후에도 많은 사람들이 나무 심기 운동을 지속하며 그녀의 뜻을 이어가고 있어요!

환경 운동의 루키, 그레타 툰베리(Greta Thunberg)

그레타 툰베리는 스웨덴의 환경 운동가로, 어린 시절부터 기후변화에 관심이 많았어요. 2018년 여름, 스웨덴의 폭염을 겪으며 환경 운동의 필요성을 깨닫게 되죠. 그녀는 15살의 어린 나이에도 불구하고, 스웨덴 수도의 국회의사당 앞에서 기후 변화 대책 마련을 촉구하는 1인 시위를 벌였어요. 매주 금요일마다 학교에 가지 않고 시위를 했는데, 이 시위는 이후 세계적인 기후 운동인 '미래를 위한 금요일(Fridays for Future, FFF)'로 발전하게 되죠. 전 세계 수백만 명의 학생들이 툰베리와 같이 등교를 거부하고 기후 재앙에 반대하는 시위에 동참했어요.

이후 툰베리는 2019년 9월 23일 미국 뉴욕에서 열린 유엔 기후행동 정상회의에 참석하기 위해 탄소 배출을 하지 않는 태양광 요트를 이용해 대서양을 건넜고, 이 때문에 많은 주목을 받기도 했죠!

우리도 툰베리처럼 환경을 위해 작은 실천부터 시작해 보면 어떨까요?

www.nebooks.co.kr

Section

9

VOCABULARY

through 젠 ~을 통해

opening 명 구멍, 틈

act 명 행위; *동 역할[기능]을
하다

sense 명 감각 동 느끼다, 감
지하다

powerful 형 강력한

human 명 인간

locate 동 (~의 위치를) 찾아
내다

pick up ~을 알아채다

weak 형 약한, 희미한

far away 멀리 (떨어져)

drop 명 (액체의) 방울

huge 형 거대한, 막대한

amount 명 총액; *양

seawater 명 해수, 바닷물

ability 명 능력

문제

attract 동 끌어들이다

lastly 부 마지막으로, 끝으로

Can fish smell? The answer is yes. A fish can smell through two or four openings in its head. These openings, called *nares, act much in the same way as our noses do. In fact, some fish have a sense of smell that is 500 times more powerful than a human's! This strong sense of smell helps fish locate food, sense danger, or find their way home. Fish can pick up even very weak smells in the water. _____, sharks can smell blood from far away, even if there is only one drop of blood in a huge amount of seawater. The sense of smell is one of a fish's most important abilities.

*nares 콧구멍

1 글의 제목으로 가장 적절한 것은?

① Fish Are Able to Smell
② Smells That Attract Fish
③ Sharks' Amazing Sense of Smell
④ A Fish's Surprising Ability to Survive
⑤ Why Fish Have Holes in Their Head

2 글의 빈칸에 들어갈 말로 가장 알맞은 것은?

① Fortunately   ② For example
③ However   ④ In addition
⑤ Lastly

SOCIETY

02 ★☆☆
126 words

VOCABULARY

sign 몡 표지판
college 몡 대학
professor 몡 교수
parking space 주차장
disability 몡 장애
symbol 몡 상징(물)
static 혱 정적인
strengthen 통 강화하다
stereotype 몡 고정 관념
active 혱 활동적인
wheelchair 몡 휠체어
view A as B A를 B로 여기다 [생각하다]
tool 몡 도구
feature 통 특징으로 삼다
officially 뫼 공식적으로, 정식으로
adopt 통 채택하다
perception 몡 인식, 지각

Are there any signs that you would like to change? In Boston, an artist and a college professor decided to change the sign for parking spaces for people with disabilities. They thought the symbol in the old sign was too static. They believed that it could strengthen the stereotype that people with disabilities are not active. They wanted people to view wheelchairs simply as tools that help people with disabilities. So they created a new design featuring a person in a moving wheelchair. Then they started putting stickers with the new design all over Boston. Soon, cities such as New York and Hartford officially adopted this image. The cities hoped that the sign would change people's perceptions of people with disabilities. Which city will be next?

1 글의 제목으로 가장 적절한 것은?

① How to Make Good Signs
② Examples of Interesting Signs
③ The People Who Make Signs
④ Reasons to Change Signs
⑤ Changing Signs, Changing Perceptions

서술형

2 예술가와 교수가 기존의 장애인 주차 표지판을 어떻게 생각했는지 우리말로 쓰시오.

_____

🔖 VOCABULARY
carry 통 갖고 다니다
fall apart 너덜너덜해지다
fall off 떨어져 나가다
fix 통 고치다, 수리하다
collect 통 모으다, 수집하다
donation 명 기부, 기증
part 명 부분; *부품
donate 통 기부하다, 기증하다
serious 형 진지한
purpose 명 목적
aware of ~을 알고 있는, 의식하는
damaged 형 손상된
donor 명 기부자, 기증자
rate 명 비율
come to an end 끝나다
attention 명 주목, 관심
awareness 명 의식, 지각

🔖 VOCA PLUS
장기와 관련된 어휘
organ 명 장기
lung 명 폐
heart 명 심장
stomach 명 위
liver 명 간
kidney 명 신장, 콩팥

Many children have a favorite doll or toy ⓐ that they carry everywhere. Over time, however, these toys begin to fall apart. Eyes get lost, and arms fall off. For a child, this can be very sad. That's why two workers in Tokyo ⓑ starting a campaign to fix these toys. They collected old toys through donations. Then they fixed the children's toys with parts from the ⓒ donated toys. The campaign also had a more serious purpose. Not enough people in Japan donate organs. The campaign wanted to make people aware of this problem. By finding new parts for damaged toys, the workers hoped ⓓ to increase the organ donor rates in their country. The campaign has come to an end now. But it gained global attention and succeeded in ⓔ increasing awareness about the importance of organ donations.

90

1 글의 주제로 가장 알맞은 것은?

① 잃어버린 장난감을 찾아 주는 기관
② 아이에게 맞는 장난감을 고르는 방법
③ 새로운 장기 이식술을 개발한 의사들
④ 아픈 아이들에게 장난감을 만들어 주는 회사
⑤ 장난감을 고쳐 주고 장기 기증을 장려하는 캠페인

2 Which is NOT grammatically correct among ⓐ~ⓔ?

① ⓐ   ② ⓑ   ③ ⓒ   ④ ⓓ   ⑤ ⓔ

서술형

3 글의 밑줄 친 this problem이 의미하는 것이 무엇인지 본문에서 찾아 우리말로 간단히 쓰시오.

_____

서술형

4 다음 영영 뜻풀이에 해당하는 단어를 본문에서 찾아 쓰시오.

to gather a lot of something

_____

✎ **VOCABULARY**

hit (동) 치다, 때리다; *닿다
sense (동) 느끼다, 감지하다
outside (형) 외부의
temperature (명) 온도
control (동) 조절하다, 조정하다
difference (명) 차이
environment (명) 환경
depending on ~에 따라
either A or B A 또는 B (중 하나)
sensitive (형) 예민한
average (형) 평균의
degree (명) (온도계의) 도
gap (명) 차이, 격차

✎ **VOCA PLUS**

다의어 **spot**

1. (명) (작은) 점, 반점
   He has a spot on his face.

2. (명) (지저분한) 얼룩
   I found a small spot on my shirt.

3. (명) (특정한) 곳, 자리, 부위
   a weak spot
   a hot spot

4. (동) 발견하다, 알아채다
   I spotted you in the crowd.

You are about to wash your hair on a cold day. When you touch the water with your hand, it feels warm. But when it hits your head, it feels very cold. Why is this? It's because you have cold and warm spots on your skin. These spots sense the outside temperature and control changes in your skin's temperature. (a) Because of this, the temperature difference between your skin and the outside environment is important. (b) Depending on your skin's temperature, the same outside temperature can feel either warm or cold. (c) So some people are more sensitive to warm or cold temperatures. (d) The average temperature of a person's hands is 31 degrees *Celsius. (e) But the average temperature of a person's head is 36 degrees Celsius. On a cold day, this gap becomes even bigger because your hands get colder more quickly than your head does. So, in the winter, the same water can feel cold on your head, but warm on your hands.

*Celsius 섭씨의

1   What is this passage mainly about?

① 외부의 자극에 민감한 신체 부위
② 겨울에 체온을 잘 유지하는 방법
③ 신체에서 냉점과 온점이 하는 역할
④ 인간의 몸이 느낄 수 있는 감각의 종류
⑤ 손과 머리가 온도를 다르게 느끼는 이유

2   문장 (a)~(e) 중 글의 흐름과 관계가 <u>없는</u> 것은?

① (a)   ② (b)   ③ (c)   ④ (d)   ⑤ (e)

서술형

3   피부의 냉점과 온점이 하는 일을 본문에서 찾아 우리말로 쓰시오. (2가지)

(1) _____

(2) _____

서술형

4   글의 내용과 일치하도록 빈칸에 알맞은 말을 본문에서 찾아 쓰시오.

> The average temperature of our hands is five degrees Celsius _____ than that of our head. This gap gets _____ on cold days.

Talk Talk한
이야기
p. 95

REVIEW TEST

정답 및 해설 p. 36

A 다음 의미에 해당하는 단어를 | 보기 |에서 찾아 쓰시오.

| 보기 | donate   adopt   passive   locate   control

1 _____: not acting to change a situation

2 _____: to find out where something is

3 _____: to give something to help others

4 _____: to formally accept and start to use something

5 _____: to influence or limit the way something acts or works

B 다음 밑줄 친 단어와 의미가 비슷한 것을 고르시오.

1 He <u>sensed</u> that something was wrong.

   ① felt   ② accepted   ③ escaped   ④ described   ⑤ improved

2 My brother <u>fixed</u> this laptop.

   ① bought   ② lent   ③ borrowed   ④ repaired   ⑤ broke

3 The <u>gap</u> between the rich and the poor is getting bigger.

   ① similarity   ② choice   ③ degree   ④ difference   ⑤ relationship

C 우리말과 같은 뜻이 되도록 빈칸에 들어갈 말을 | 보기 |에서 골라 알맞은 형태로 쓰시오.

| 보기 | fall apart   search for   pick up

1 그 개는 숲에서 주인의 냄새를 알아차렸다.

The dog _____ its owner's scent in the forest.

2 나는 보고서를 위한 정보를 찾아보느라 밤을 샜다.

I stayed up all night to _____ information for my report.

3 아빠의 낡은 차가 부서지기 시작했다.

My dad's old car started _____.

Talk Talk한 이야기

피부의 감각점

최근에 종이에 손가락을 베였어…! 상처는 잘 보이지도 않는데 왜 이렇게 아픈 거람.

그건 손톱에 감각점이 없기 때문이야! 반대로 손끝에는 감각점이 많이 분포하고 있지. 그래서 작은 자극에도 훨씬 아팠을 거야.
점자책을 손끝으로 읽는 이유도 이 부위의 감각이 예민하기 때문이지.

그런 이유가 있었다니.. 그런데 감각점이 뭐야?

감각점은 압력, 온도 변화와 같은 외부 자극을 느끼는 감각을 의미해.
감각점의 종류로는 통점(열, 강한 압력 감지), 압점(압력 감지), 촉점 (접촉 감지), 냉점(온도 하강 감지), 온점(온도 상승 감지)이 있어!
감각점 덕분에 우린 뜨겁거나 뾰족한 물체에 닿았을 때 빠르게 반응해서 우리 몸을 보호할 수 있지.

아하! 겨울에 너무 추우면 손끝이랑 발끝, 심지어 귀조차도 차갑다 못해 아프기까지 하던데 이것도 감각점과 관련이 있을까?

관련이 있지! 특히 압점, 온점, 냉점은 자극이 심하면 몸에서 통각으로 받아들이거든. 그리고 흥미롭게도 우리 몸에는 평균적으로 냉점이 온점보다 많이 분포해 있기도 해.

정말? 그럼 우리 몸은 더위보다 추위를 더 잘 타겠네.
어쩐지 목욕탕에 가면 온탕보다 냉탕에 있기가 더 어렵더라

www.nebooks.co.kr

Section

10

VOCABULARY

countless ⑱ 무수한, 셀 수 없이 많은

designate ⑧ 지정하다

annual ⑲ 매년의

influence ⑧ 영향을 미치다

industry ⑲ 산업

matching ⑲ 어울리는, 조화 되는

identify ⑧ 식별하다

over ㉮ ~이 넘는

solid color 단색

unique ⑲ 고유의, 독특한

cosmetics ⑲ 화장품

printer ⑲ 프린터; *인쇄업자

instead of ~ 대신에

exact ⑲ 정확한

【문제】

unusual ⑲ 특이한, 드문

advantage ⑲ 이점, 장점

identification ⑲ 식별

Although there are countless different colors, there is a company that designates one special color each year. The company is called Pantone. Its annual "color of the year" influences many decisions in the fashion and beauty industries. Pantone is also known for its color matching system. The company has identified over 2,000 different solid colors. Each color has been given its own unique number. This system is very helpful for cosmetics companies, fashion designers, web designers, printers, and other professionals. For example, instead of calling a color "dark red," they can call it "19-1664." This allows everyone to know the exact color they're talking about.

1 글의 제목으로 가장 적절한 것은?

① An Unusual Job: Naming Colors

② The Most Popular Color of All Time

③ The Process of Inventing a New Color

④ The Advantages of a Color Matching System

⑤ A Company That Made a Color Identification System

서술형

2 밑줄 친 This system이 가리키는 것이 무엇인지 우리말로 간단히 쓰시오.

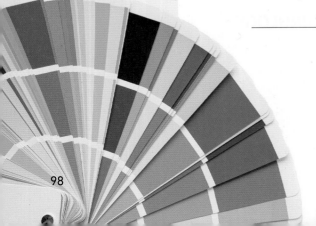

98

WORLD

02 ★☆☆
124 words

VOCABULARY

section ⑲ 부분; *(시·군의) 구역

located ⑲ (~에) 위치한

steep ⑲ 가파른

hillside ⑲ (작은 산·언덕의) 비탈

resident ⑲ 거주자, 주민

step ⑲ 걸음; *계단

travel ⑧ 여행하다; *이동하다

construction ⑲ 건설, 공사

outdoor ⑲ 야외의

free ⑲ 무료의

protect ⑧ 보호하다

solution ⑲ 해결책

official ⑲ 공식적인 *⑲ 공무원

eventually ⑨ 마침내, 결국

add ⑧ 추가하다

roof ⑲ 지붕

for the better 보다 나은 쪽으로

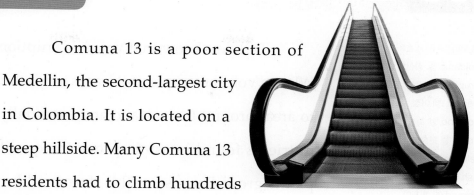

Comuna 13 is a poor section of Medellin, the second-largest city in Colombia. It is located on a steep hillside. Many Comuna 13 residents had to climb hundreds of steps every day just to travel to and from their homes. But not anymore. Thanks to the construction of a 384-meter-long outdoor escalator, they can now easily travel up and down the hill. This useful escalator is free to ride. Before it was built, (<u>walk, 35 minutes, it, to, took</u>) to the top. But now it's possible to do so in six minutes. At first, people using the escalator weren't protected from the rain or hot sun. As a solution, city officials eventually added an orange roof. A simple escalator changed Medellin for the better!

1 Comuna 13의 에스컬레이터에 관한 설명 중 글의 내용과 일치하지 <u>않는</u> 것은?

① 콜롬비아에서 두 번째로 크다.

② 길이는 380미터가 넘는다.

③ 무료로 이용할 수 있다.

④ 6분 만에 언덕 정상에 도착한다.

⑤ 비 혹은 뜨거운 볕을 막아주는 지붕이 있다.

서술형

2 글의 ( ) 안에 주어진 단어를 바르게 배열하여 문장을 완성하시오.

_____

📝 **VOCABULARY**

volcanic (형) 화산의

eruption (명) 폭발, 분출

benefit (명) 이점, 이로움

volcano (명) 화산

erupt (동) 분출하다

release (동) 방출하다, 내뿜다

ash (명) 재

spread (동) 퍼지다

soil (명) 땅; 흙

nutrient (명) 영양소, 영양분

quality (명) 질, 품질

below (전) ~ 아래에

ground (명) 지면, 땅

hot spring 온천

significant (형) 중요한;
*커다란, 상당한

burn (명) 화상

what's more 더구나, 게다가

electricity (명) 전기

📝 **VOCA PLUS**

다의어 land

1. (명) 육지, 땅
   He owns a lot of land.

2. (동) 착륙하다
   The plane landed
   safely.

3. (동) 떨어지다
   A boy fell and landed
   on the floor.

Did you know that volcanic eruptions have many benefits? When a volcano erupts, it releases ash into the air. The ash spreads to areas around the volcano and eventually lands on the soil. The nutrients found in ash improve the quality of the soil and help plants grow. Because of this, farmers like to live near *dormant volcanoes. (a) Another benefit of volcanoes is that they produce a lot of heat and energy. (b) When the heat is below ground, it helps to create hot springs. (c) Water in some hot springs can be so hot that it can cause significant burns. (d) What's more, many countries around the world have even begun to use volcanic energy to make electricity. (e) The most important benefit of all is that volcanoes have produced most of the Earth's air and water. Volcanoes make it possible for us to live on Earth!

*dormant volcano 휴화산

1   What is this passage mainly about?

     ① 화산 폭발의 징후

     ② 화산 폭발의 위험성

     ③ 화산의 긍정적인 측면

     ④ 화산 폭발 시 대피 방법

     ⑤ 화산 폭발로 생성되는 물질

2   화산 활동이 만들어 내는 것으로 언급되지 <u>않은</u> 것은?

     ① 화산재   ② 비료

     ③ 열 에너지   ④ 공기

     ⑤ 물

3   문장 (a)~(e) 중 글의 흐름과 관계가 <u>없는</u> 것은?

     ① (a)   ② (b)   ③ (c)   ④ (d)   ⑤ (e)

서술형

4   글의 밑줄 친 <u>this</u>가 가리키는 것을 본문에서 찾아 우리말로 쓰시오.

_____

🖋 VOCABULARY

electric car 전기차
opinion (명) 의견
smoothly (부) 부드럽게
noise (명) 소음
gas-powered 휘발유로
움직이는
gas station 주유소
overnight (부) 밤사이에,
하룻밤 동안
unlike (전) ~와는 달리
pollute (동) 오염시키다
inconvenient (형) 불편한
compared to ~와 비교하여
charging station 충전소
available (형) 이용 가능한
road trip 장거리 자동차 여행
worth (명) 가치; *(얼마) 어치
fill up ~을 가득 채우다

🖋 VOCA PLUS

다의어 charge

1. (동) 청구하다
   The restaurant charged
   us $25 for the pasta.

2. (동) 충전하다
   Before use, the battery
   must be charged.

3. (명) 요금
   We used the facilities
   free of charge.

My older sister, Suzie, is going to buy a new car. I want her to buy an electric car, but she doesn't want to. Here are our opinions about electric cars.

Me: Electric cars drive smoothly. (①) They also don't make as much noise as gas-powered cars. (②) In addition, they are very easy ⓐ to charge. (③) If you have an electric car, you don't need to go to a gas station. (④) You can just charge the car at your home overnight, and it will be ready in the morning. (⑤) Unlike gas-powered cars, electric cars don't pollute the air.

Suzie: In my opinion, electric cars are inconvenient. Compared to gas stations, there ⓑ aren't many charging stations available. So ⓒ that might be a problem when I go on road trips. Electric cars also take a long time ⓓ charging. It takes about an hour to add 40 to 45 miles' worth of electricity to an electric car. However, with a gas-powered car, ⓔ it only takes a few minutes to fill up the tank.

1 전기차에 대해 글에서 언급된 내용이 <u>아닌</u> 것은? (2가지)

① 소음의 정도　　　　　　　　② 충전 시간
③ 환경에 끼치는 영향　　　　　④ 작동 원리
⑤ 가격

2 글의 흐름으로 보아 주어진 문장이 들어갈 위치로 가장 적절한 곳은?

> They are also much better for the environment.

①　　　　　②　　　　　③　　　　　④　　　　　⑤

3 Which is NOT grammatically correct among ⓐ~ⓔ?

① ⓐ　　　　② ⓑ　　　　③ ⓒ　　　　④ ⓓ　　　　⑤ ⓔ

서술형

4 글의 내용과 일치하도록 빈칸에 알맞은 말을 | 보기 |에서 골라 쓰시오.

| 보기 |　　ready　　filling　　charged　　available　　inconvenient

Suzie believes electric cars are ＿＿＿＿＿＿＿. That's because there are not many charging stations ＿＿＿＿＿＿. What's more, an electric car needs to be ＿＿＿＿＿＿ for a long time for the battery to be full, while ＿＿＿＿＿＿ up a gas-powered car only takes a few minutes.

Talk Talk한
이야기
p. 105

REVIEW TEST

정답 및 해설 p. 40

A 다음 의미에 해당하는 단어를 | 보기 |에서 찾아 쓰시오.

| 보기 | identify   resident   release   designate   available

1 _____ : able to be used

2 _____ : to give an official name or title

3 _____ : to cause something to spread from a source

4 _____ : someone who lives in a certain place

5 _____ : to recognize and distinguish a particular thing

B 다음 밑줄 친 단어와 의미가 비슷한 것을 고르시오.

1 Light <u>travels</u> faster than sound.

① lasts   ② moves   ③ charges   ④ produces   ⑤ pollutes

2 There is an <u>annual</u> event at the library.

① unusual   ② special   ③ yearly   ④ convenient   ⑤ significant

3 There were <u>countless</u> stars in the sky.

① bright   ② many   ③ tiny   ④ shiny   ⑤ few

C 우리말과 같은 뜻이 되도록 빈칸에 들어갈 말을 | 보기 |에서 골라 알맞은 형태로 쓰시오.

| 보기 | for the better   fill up   instead of

1 그들은 택시를 타는 대신에 집에 걸어가는 것을 택했다.

They chose to walk home _____ taking a taxi.

2 세상은 좋은 쪽으로 변화해 오고 있는 것으로 보인다.

It seems that the world has been changing _____.

3 그는 병을 채우기 위해 식수대 물을 틀었다.

He turned on the water fountain to _____ his bottle.

전기차, 과연 친환경적일까?

전기 자동차와 이차전지

전기 자동차는 충전 배터리(이차 전지)를 동력으로 움직여요. 이차전지는 휴대폰 배터리처럼 방전되면 재충전해서 쓸 수 있어요. 이론적으로 전기는 원래 "깨끗하게 정제되어" 전기 자동차는 매연을 배출하지 않아요. 그러니 화석 연료 자동차에 비해 전기 자동차는 언뜻 보기에 친환경적으로 보이기도 합니다.

정말 친환경적일까?

하지만 전기는 어떻게 만들어질까요? 우리나라의 경우 수력, 풍력, 조력, 태양광 발전으로 생산되는 에너지는 약 1퍼센트에 불과해요. 약 60퍼센트는 화력 발전에, 나머지 약 40퍼센트는 원자력 발전에 의존하지요. 화력 발전은 화석 연료를 태워서 에너지를 만들어 내며, 이 과정에서 일산화탄소(CO)와 이산화탄소($CO2$)가 발생해요. 원자력 발전소에서는 방사능 폐기물이 발생하죠. 전기 자동차를 사용한다는 것은 이러한 부산물이 계속 나온다는 의미예요. 즉, 친환경적이라고 보기는 힘듭니다.

친환경이라기보다 고효율

이렇다 보니 친환경 자동차라는 명칭은 '고효율 자동차'로 바꾸는 게 더 정확해 보입니다. 고효율 자동차, 즉 똑같은 전기량으로 더 긴 주행 거리를 주행할 수 있는 자동차이지요. 당연히 부산물도 줄어들어요. 전기차 연비가 높아질수록 친환경에 더 가까워지겠죠?

Photo Credits

p. 15   Photo by Andreas Kay
        https://thespiderblog.com/?s=bunny

p. 15   Female Cyclocosmia truncata, Jason Bond
        http://working.tolweb.org/onlinecontributors/app?page=ViewImageData&service=external&sp=32300

p. 15   Cyclocosmia Ausserer
        https://commons.wikimedia.org/wiki/File:Cyclocosmia.jpg?uselang=ko

p. 15   a male peacock spider
        https://commons.wikimedia.org/wiki/File:Male_peacock_spider2.svg?uselang=ko

p. 45   United Airlines Flight 175 crashes into the south tower of the World Trade Center by Robert J. Fisch
        https://commons.wikimedia.org/wiki/File:UA_Flight_175_hits_WTC_south_tower_9-11_edit.jpeg?uselang=ko

p. 80   Photo by Sara Musashi
        https://www.robingreenfield.org/la

MEMO

MEMO

MEMO

지은이

NE능률 영어교육연구소

NE능률 영어교육연구소는 혁신적이며 효율적인 영어 교재를 개발하고
영어 학습의 질을 한 단계 높이고자 노력하는 NE능률의 연구조직입니다.

1316 Reading 〈Level 2〉

펴 낸 이	주민홍
펴 낸 곳	서울특별시 마포구 월드컵북로 396(상암동) 누리꿈스퀘어 비즈니스타워 10층
	㈜ NE능률 (우편번호 03925)
펴 낸 날	2024년 1월 5일 개정판 제1쇄 발행
	2024년 6월 15일 제3쇄
전 화	02 2014 7114
팩 스	02 3142 0356
홈 페 이 지	www.neungyule.com
등 록 번 호	제1-68호
I S B N	979-11-253-4288-5
정 가	14,000원

NE 능률

고객센터

교재 내용 문의 : contact.nebooks.co.kr (별도의 가입 절차 없이 작성 가능)

제품 구매, 교환, 불량, 반품 문의 : 02-2014-7114

☎ 전화문의는 본사 업무시간 중에만 가능합니다.

기초부터 내신까지 중학 독해 완성

1316

1316 READING

WORKBOOK

LEVEL
2

A   영어 단어에는 우리말 뜻을, 우리말 뜻에는 영어 단어를 쓰시오.

01 commonly   _____

02 phrase   _____

03 be made up of   _____

04 and so on   _____

05 conversation   _____

06 _____ 혼란스러워하는

07 _____ 발표하다, 공개하다

08 _____ 대문자로 쓰다

09 _____ 문장

10 _____ 타자 치다

B   굵게 표시된 부분에 유의하여 우리말 문장을 완성하시오.

01 **Look at the conversation** on the phone.

전화 속 _____.

02 **Are you confused by the words** *TBH*, *GOAT*, and so on?

TBH, GOAT 등의 _____?

03 That's why they **are all capitalized**.

그래서 그것들은 _____.

04 Acronyms **are commonly used** online and in text messages.

두문자어는 온라인이나 문자 메시지에 _____.

05 They **make it easy to type** short messages.

그것들은 짧은 메시지를 _____.

06 Now **try reading** the conversation again!

이제 대화를 다시 _____!

07 I forgot **it was released today**!

나는 _____ 잊었어!

A 영어 단어에는 우리말 뜻을, 우리말 뜻에는 영어 단어를 쓰시오.

01 resist _____

02 pressure _____

03 fall over _____

04 eventually _____

05 spread out _____

06 balance _____

07 _____ 들어 있다, 포함하다

08 _____ 바깥쪽으로, 밖으로

09 _____ 맨 아래 (부분), 바닥

10 _____ 증가시키다, 늘리다

11 _____ 튀어나온 부분, 돌기

12 _____ 면적

B 굵게 표시된 부분에 유의하여 우리말 문장을 완성하시오.

01 You won't find them on plastic bottles **that contain water or juice**.

_____ 페트병에서는 그것들을 찾을 수 없을 것이다.

02 The bottle **must be able to resist** this pressure.

그 병은 이 압력에 _____.

03 **If the bottle has a greater area**, there will be less pressure in it.

만약 _____, 병 속의 압력이 더 적어질 것이다.

04 That's why the bumps **are added**.

그래서 돌기가 _____ 것이다.

05 What would happen **without the bumps**?

_____ 무슨 일이 일어날까?

06 The pressure **would push** the bottom outward.

압력이 바닥을 밖으로 _____.

A 주어진 우리말과 같은 뜻이 되도록 빈칸에 알맞은 말을 | 보기 |에서 골라 쓰시오. (필요시 형태 바꾸기)

| 보기 | 　　trap　　gather　　species　　release　　breathe |

01 이 장치는 잠수부들이 호흡할 공기를 담고 있었다.

These devices held air for divers to _____.

02 그것은 물속에서 평생을 보내는 유일한 거미 종(種)이다.

It is the only _____ of spider that spends its whole life underwater.

03 그 털은 공기 방울을 가두는 것을 돕는다.

The hairs help _____ the bubbles.

04 그 거미는 이 공기 방울을 거미줄로 가져와 풀어 놓는다.

The spider brings these bubbles to the web and _____ them.

05 시간이 지나면서, 거미는 더 많은 공기 방울을 모아야 한다.

Over time, the spider must _____ more bubbles.

B 우리말 문장을 보고 주어진 영어 단어를 이용하여 문장을 완성하시오.

01 사람들은 물속에 들어가기 위해 잠수종을 사용했다. (go, underwater)

People used diving bells _____ _____ _____.

02 이 장치는 종과 같은 모양이었다. (shape, a bell)

These devices _____ _____ _____ _____ _____.

03 그것은 자신의 다리와 배를 사용하여 공기 방울을 모은다.(use, leg)

It collects air bubbles _____ _____ _____ and belly.

04 그 공기 방울은 안에서 살기에 충분히 크다. (big, enough, live)

The bubble is _____ _____ _____ _____ in.

05 그것은 자신의 생애 대부분을 공기 방울 집에서 살며 보낸다. (spend, its life, live)

It _____ _____ _____ _____ _____

inside its bubble house.

A 주어진 우리말과 같은 뜻이 되도록 빈칸에 알맞은 말을 | 보기 |에서 골라 쓰시오. (필요시 형태 바꾸기)

| 보기 |　border　　exchange　　trade　　attention　　impressed

01 그는 종이를 끼우는 클립에서 집으로 교환했다.

He _____ up from a paper clip to a house.

02 그녀는 크게 감명받았고 같은 것을 해 보기로 결심했다.

She was greatly _____ and decided to try the same thing.

03 우선, 그녀는 머리핀을 귀걸이 한 쌍으로 바꾸었다.

First, she _____ a hairpin for a pair of earrings.

04 그것은 많은 관심을 받았다.

It got lots of _____.

05 하지만 그것을 국경을 넘어 가지고 오는 것은 어려웠다.

But it was hard to bring it across the _____.

B 우리말 문장을 보고 주어진 영어 단어를 이용하여 문장을 완성하시오.

01 머리핀으로 새집의 값을 지불하는 것이 가능한가? (possible, pay)

_____ _____ _____ _____ _____ for a new house

with a hairpin?

02 그것은 Demi Skipper라는 이름의 한 미국 여성이 한 일이다. (name, do)

That's what an American woman _____ _____ _____

_____.

03 그녀는 그 귀걸이를 네 쌍의 안경과 맞바꾸었다. (trade, the earrings, glasses)

She _____ _____ _____ _____ _____ _____.

04 물물 교환 상대를 찾기가 더 어려워졌다. (become, hard, find)

It _____ _____ _____ _____ trading partners.

05 그녀가 그것을 미국으로 들여오는 데 5개월이 걸렸다. (take, get)

It _____ _____ _____ _____ _____ _____

_____ it into the US.

본책 p. 18　　　　이름

A 영어 단어에는 우리말 뜻을, 우리말 뜻에는 영어 단어를 쓰시오.

01 mild ＿＿＿＿＿＿＿＿＿　　　　**08** ＿＿＿＿＿＿＿＿ 양식

02 staff ＿＿＿＿＿＿＿＿＿　　　　**09** ＿＿＿＿＿＿＿＿ (비용이) ~이다

03 below ＿＿＿＿＿＿＿＿＿　　　　**10** ＿＿＿＿＿＿＿＿ 진행

04 afterward ＿＿＿＿＿＿＿＿＿　　　　**11** ＿＿＿＿＿＿＿＿ 마감 시간, 기한

05 fill out ＿＿＿＿＿＿＿＿＿　　　　**12** ＿＿＿＿＿＿＿＿ 이용할 수 있는

06 meet ＿＿＿＿＿＿＿＿＿　　　　**13** ＿＿＿＿＿＿＿＿ 무제한의

07 normal ＿＿＿＿＿＿＿＿＿　　　　**14** ＿＿＿＿＿＿＿＿ 압력, 압박

B 굵게 표시된 부분에 유의하여 우리말 문장을 완성하시오.

01 Do you have **a deadline to meet**?

당신은 ＿＿＿＿＿＿＿＿＿＿＿＿＿＿＿＿＿＿＿＿＿＿＿＿＿＿ 있습니까?

02 When you enter, you fill out a form **with the time you need**.

당신은 입장할 때 ＿＿＿＿＿＿＿＿＿＿＿＿＿＿＿＿＿ 양식을 작성합니다.

03 You choose **the amount of pressure you want**.

당신은 ＿＿＿＿＿＿＿＿＿＿＿＿＿＿＿＿＿＿＿＿＿＿＿＿ 선택합니다.

04 "Normal" means **they will check it hourly**.

'Normal'은 ＿＿＿＿＿＿＿＿＿＿＿＿＿＿＿＿＿＿＿＿＿＿＿ 의미입니다.

05 They **will keep watching you** until you finish your work.

그들은 당신이 일을 마칠 때까지 ＿＿＿＿＿＿＿＿＿＿＿＿＿＿＿＿＿.

06 Free Wi-Fi **is provided**.

무료 와이파이가 ＿＿＿＿＿＿＿＿＿＿＿＿＿＿＿＿＿＿＿＿＿＿＿.

A 영어 단어에는 우리말 뜻을, 우리말 뜻에는 영어 단어를 쓰시오.

01 snowflake _____   08 _____ 빈, 비어 있는

02 disappear _____   09 _____ 녹다

03 calm _____   10 _____ 실제로

04 instead _____   11 _____ 반사하다

05 side _____   12 _____ 표면

06 completely _____   13 _____ 얼다

07 absorb _____   14 _____ 음파

B 굵게 표시된 부분에 유의하여 우리말 문장을 완성하시오.

01 Why do snowy nights **seem so calm and peaceful**?

왜 눈 내리는 밤은 _____?

02 It's because snow **makes everything quieter**!

왜냐하면 눈이 _____ 때문이다!

03 The shape of snowflakes **makes this possible**.

눈송이의 모양이 _____.

04 **As the snow melts**, the spaces in the snowflakes **get smaller**.

_____ 눈송이 속의 공간은 _____.

05 This actually **makes sounds seem louder**.

이것은 실제로 _____.

06 **When the snow starts to melt**, the special feeling will disappear.

_____, 그 특별한 느낌은 사라질 것이다.

A 주어진 우리말과 같은 뜻이 되도록 빈칸에 알맞은 말을 | 보기 |에서 골라 쓰시오. (필요시 형태 바꾸기)

| 보기 | letter   customer   curved   symbol   represent

01 로고는 회사의 고유한 상징이다.

A logo is the unique _____ of a company.

02 화살표가 글자 'a'에서 시작한다.

The arrow starts at the _____ *a*.

03 화살표가 구부러져 있다.

The arrow is _____.

04 이것은 Amazon이 고객들을 행복하게 해 주고 싶어 한다는 것을 의미한다.

This means that Amazon wants to make _____ happy.

05 그 점들은 회사의 세 개의 본점을 나타낸다.

The dots _____ the company's original three stores.

B 우리말 문장을 보고 주어진 영어 단어를 이용하여 문장을 완성하시오.

01 로고를 통해, 회사는 자기가 어떤 회사인지 보여 준다. (what)

Through its logo, a company shows _____ _____ _____.

02 그 화살표는 마치 미소처럼 보인다. (look, a smile)

The arrow _____ _____ _____ _____.

03 세계에서 가장 큰 피자 회사인 Domino's는 독특한 로고를 가지고 있다. (large, company)

Domino's, _____ _____ _____ _____ in the world, has
a unique logo.

04 Domino's는 모든 새로운 가게에 점을 추가하길 원했다.(add, a dot)

Domino's _____ _____ _____ _____ _____ for
every new store.

05 그 회사는 자신의 생각을 바꿨다. (mind)

The company _____ _____ _____.

A 주어진 우리말과 같은 뜻이 되도록 빈칸에 알맞은 말을 | 보기 |에서 골라 쓰시오. (필요시 형태 바꾸기)

| 보기 |　　　　run　　dish　　dough　　tender　　flip

01 Stéphanie는 프랑스에서 여동생과 함께 호텔을 운영했다.

Stéphanie _____ a hotel with her sister in France.

02 그녀가 가장 잘하는 요리는 사과 타르트였다.

Her best _____ was an apple tart.

03 그녀의 타르트는 부드럽고 달콤했다.

Her tart was _____ and sweet.

04 그녀는 그냥 얇게 썬 사과 조각 위에 반죽을 올렸다!

She simply put the _____ on top of the sliced apples!

05 그녀는 그저 타르트를 거꾸로 뒤집었다.

She just _____ the tarte upside down.

B 우리말 문장을 보고 주어진 영어 단어를 이용하여 문장을 완성하시오.

01 Stéphanie는 호텔에서 주방장으로 일했다. (work, a chef)

Stéphanie _____ _____ _____ _____ in the hotel.

02 그녀에게 좋은 생각이 떠올랐다. (come)

She _____ _____ _____ a bright idea.

03 이러한 방식으로 타르트를 굽는 것은 그 사과들이 설탕을 더 잘 흡수하도록 도왔다. (absorb)

Baking it in this way _____ _____ _____ _____ the sugar better.

04 Stéphanie의 새 타르트는 그 어느 때보다 맛이 더 풍부하고 달콤했다! (rich, sweet, ever)

Stéphanie's new tart tasted _____ _____ _____ _____ _____!

05 그것이 타르트 타탱이 탄생한 순간이었다. (the moment, born)

That was _____ _____ tarte Tatin _____ _____.

A 영어 단어에는 우리말 뜻을, 우리말 뜻에는 영어 단어를 쓰시오.

01 slippery _____
02 soil _____
03 stream _____
04 melt _____
05 cause _____
06 heating wire _____
07 flow _____
08 harm _____

09 _____ 해가 없는, 무해한
10 _____ ~이 들어 있다
11 _____ 화학 물질
12 _____ 미끄러지다
13 _____ 화산의
14 _____ 광물(질)
15 _____ 보도, 인도
16 _____ 막다, 방지하다

B 굵게 표시된 부분에 유의하여 우리말 문장을 완성하시오.

01 De-icing products **allow us to safely walk on sidewalks**.

제설제는 _____.

02 They contain chemicals **that are bad for the soil**.

그것들은 _____ 화학 물질을 포함하고 있다.

03 These chemicals **can cause problems for fish**.

이런 화학 물질은 _____.

04 People **have made alternatives** to these harmful chemicals.

사람들은 이러한 해로운 화학 물질의 _____.

05 One example is a type of road with heating wires **that can melt snow and ice**.

한 가지 예는 _____ 전열선이 있는 도로의 형태이다.

06 It **prevents people and cars from sliding** on slippery roads.

그것은 _____ 미끄러운 도로에서 _____.

A   영어 단어에는 우리말 뜻을, 우리말 뜻에는 영어 단어를 쓰시오.

01 cheap _____

02 discounted _____

03 consumer _____

04 occur _____

05 above _____

06 as a result _____

07 receive _____

08 _____ 원래의, 본래의

09 _____ 효과

10 _____ 상상하다

11 _____ 비싼

12 _____ 경험하다

13 _____ ~에 근거하여

14 _____ 다시 말해서, 즉

B   굵게 표시된 부분에 유의하여 우리말 문장을 완성하시오.

01 **Imagine you go shopping and find** cool shoes for $150.

_____ 150달러짜리의 멋진 신발을 _____.

02 You **have just experienced** the anchoring effect!

당신은 _____ 닻 내림 효과를 _____!

03 People make decisions **based on the first information they receive**.

사람들은 _____ 결정을 내린다.

04 Stores show **the discounted price above the original price**.

상점들은 _____ 보여 준다.

05 It **makes the discounted price seem better**.

그것은 _____.

06 Consumers **are more likely to buy** the item.

소비자들은 그 상품을 _____.

A 주어진 우리말과 같은 뜻이 되도록 빈칸에 알맞은 말을 | 보기 |에서 골라 쓰시오. (필요시 형태 바꾸기)

| 보기 | remove   survive   feather   uncommon   nutrient

01 백색증은 흔하지 않은 질환이다.

Albinism is a(n) _____ condition.

02 그들은 백색 피부, 털, 그리고 깃털들을 가지고 있다.

They have white skin, hair, and _____.

03 그것들이 주변의 나무로부터 영양분들을 빼앗는다.

They take _____ from the trees around them.

04 그것들은 흙에서 독소를 제거한다.

They _____ toxins from the soil.

05 그 지역의 모든 나무는 살아남을 수 있다.

All of the trees in the area can _____.

B 우리말 문장을 보고 주어진 영어 단어를 이용하여 문장을 완성하시오.

01 그것은 사람과 동물 모두에게 발병한다. (people, animals)

It affects _____ _____ _____ _____.

02 식물 역시 백색증이 발병할 수 있다! (can, affect)

Plants _____ _____ _____ _____ albinism as well!

03 그것들은 엽록소를 가지고 있지 않은데, 그것(엽록소)은 식물이 영양분을 만드는 것을 돕는다. (help, plants)

They don't have any chlorophyll, _____ _____ _____ _____ nutrients.

04 그것들은 겨울에 갈색으로 변하는 흰색 잎을 가지고 있다. (that, turn)

They have white leaves _____ _____ _____ _____.

05 이는 그것들이 영양분을 얻게 해 준다. (allow, get)

This _____ _____ _____ _____ the nutrients.

A 주어진 우리말과 같은 뜻이 되도록 빈칸에 알맞은 말을 | 보기 |에서 골라 쓰시오. (필요시 형태 바꾸기)

| 보기 | scene   store   capture   observe   invent

01 화가들은 그들의 물감을 돼지 방광에 보관했다.

Artists _____ their paint in pig bladders.

02 이것은 화가들이 야외의 풍경들을 그리는 것을 어렵게 만들었다.

This made it difficult for artists to paint outdoor _____.

03 그는 단단한 뚜껑이 있는 금속 튜브를 발명했다.

He _____ metal tubes with hard lids.

04 밖에서 작업할 때, 그들은 더 많은 세부적인 것들을 관찰할 수 있었다.

When they worked outside, they could _____ more details.

05 그 화가들은 그것들을 캔버스에 담았다.

The artists _____ them on their canvas.

B 우리말 문장을 보고 주어진 영어 단어를 이용하여 문장을 완성하시오.

01 하지만 방광들은 가지고 다니기 어려웠다. (hard, carry)

But the bladders _____ _____ _____ _____.

02 그들은 자신들의 작업실로 돌아와야 했다. (have, return)

They _____ _____ _____ _____ their studios.

03 그들은 그들이 본 것을 기억하려고 애썼다. (try, remember)

They _____ _____ _____ what they had seen.

04 이 튜브 덕분에, 화가들은 어디서든 그림을 그릴 수 있었다. (thank, tubes)

_____ _____ _____ _____, artists could paint anywhere.

05 Claude Monet는 가장 유명한 인상주의 화가 중 한 명이다. (famous, impressionist)

Claude Monet is _____ _____ _____ _____ _____

_____.

A 영어 단어에는 우리말 뜻을, 우리말 뜻에는 영어 단어를 쓰시오.

01	airline	_____	08	_____ 제복
02	scent	_____	09	_____ 원산지의, 토박이의
03	clearly	_____	10	_____ 특정한, 특유의
04	signature	_____	11	_____ 기억
05	powerful	_____	12	_____ 비행기 승무원
06	grill	_____	13	_____ 승객
07	have an effect on	_____	14	_____ 통풍구, 환기구

B 굵게 표시된 부분에 유의하여 우리말 문장을 완성하시오.

01 Some companies use specific scents **to stay in the minds of customers**.

　　몇몇 회사들은 _____ 특정한 향기를 사용한다.

02 They used six kinds of flowers **that are native to Singapore**.

　　그들은 _____ 여섯 종류의 꽃을 사용했다.

03 The scent **is used on flight attendant uniforms**.

　　그 향기는 _____.

04 Burger King uses its vents **to spread the smell** of grilling burgers.

　　Burger King은 버거를 굽는 _____ 통풍구를 이용한다.

05 This **makes people** nearby **feel hungry**.

　　이것은 근처에 있는 _____.

06 Companies **have learned** the power of scents!

　　기업들은 향기의 위력을 _____!

A 영어 단어에는 우리말 뜻을, 우리말 뜻에는 영어 단어를 쓰시오.

01	normal	_____	07	_____ 기능
02	recognize	_____	08	_____ 유용한
03	probably	_____	09	_____ 생존하다, 살아남다
04	everyday	_____	10	_____ ~을 보다
05	regularly	_____	11	_____ 경험; 경험하다
06	object	_____	12	_____ ~에게 몰래 다가가다

B 굵게 표시된 부분에 유의하여 우리말 문장을 완성하시오.

01 **Have** you **ever seen** a face in the clouds?

당신은 구름 속에서 얼굴을 _____?

02 It **causes people to see faces** in everyday objects.

그것은 _____ 일상적인 물건에서 _____.

03 It **helped us survive** long ago.

그것은 오래 전에 _____.

04 **Being able to recognize faces** in the dark was a useful skill.

어둠 속에 있는 _____ 유용한 기술이었다.

05 It **prevented our enemies from sneaking up** on us.

그것은 _____ 우리에게 _____.

06 Our brain **regularly tries to put parts together** to form a full image.

우리의 뇌는 완전한 이미지를 형성하기 위해 _____.

본책 p. 40   이름

A 주어진 우리말과 같은 뜻이 되도록 빈칸에 알맞은 말을 | 보기 |에서 골라 쓰시오. (필요시 형태 바꾸기)

| 보기 | drain   end up   absorb   modern   unfortunately

01 많은 현대의 목욕 제품에 작은 플라스틱 조각이 들어 있다.

Many _____ bath products contain small pieces of plastic.

02 유감스럽게도, 이 작은 구슬들은 큰 문제를 일으켜 왔다.

_____, these small beads have caused big problems.

03 당신이 씻을 때 마이크로비즈는 화장실 하수구로 내려간다.

As you wash, microbeads go down the bathroom _____.

04 결국 그것들은 호수, 강, 바다로 (흘러 들어)가게 된다.

Eventually, they _____ in lakes, rivers, and oceans.

05 그곳에서 그것들은 물 속에 있는 위험한 화학 물질을 흡수한다.

There, they _____ dangerous chemicals in the water.

B 우리말 문장을 보고 주어진 영어 단어를 이용하여 문장을 완성하시오.

01 이런 마이크로비즈는 보통 폭이 2밀리미터도 안 된다. (usually, less)

These microbeads _____ _____ _____ _____ two millimeters wide.

02 그것들은 사람들이 더 깨끗하다고 느끼도록 돕는다. (feel, clean)

They _____ _____ _____ _____.

03 해산물을 먹는 사람들이 마이크로비즈에 의해 해를 입을 수 있다. (could, harm)

People who eat seafood _____ _____ _____ _____ microbeads.

04 미국은 2015년에 기업들이 마이크로비즈를 사용하는 것을 금지했다. (ban, use)

The United States _____ _____ _____ _____ microbeads in 2015.

05 그것들에 마이크로비즈가 들어 있는지 확인해 봐라. (if, contain, microbeads)

Check _____ _____ _____ _____.

16

A 주어진 우리말과 같은 뜻이 되도록 빈칸에 알맞은 말을 | 보기 |에서 골라 쓰시오. (필요시 형태 바꾸기)

| 보기 | local   empty   volunteer   organization   immediately

01 Anthony는 도와주기 위해 즉시 이라크의 바그다드로 날아갔다.

Anthony _____ flew to Baghdad, Iraq, to help.

02 바그다드 동물원에서 그는 수많은 텅 빈 우리를 발견했다.

At the Baghdad Zoo, he found many _____ cages.

03 동물원 사육사와 지역 주민들 모두가 도와주기로 했다.

Both zookeepers and _____ people agreed to help.

04 그들은 동물원의 경비로 자원했다.

They _____ as guards for the zoo.

05 국제기구들이 동물원에 보급품과 돈을 보냈다.

International _____ sent supplies and money to the zoo.

B 우리말 문장을 보고 주어진 영어 단어를 이용하여 문장을 완성하시오.

01 그 나라의 가장 큰 동물원에 있는 동물들이 죽어가고 있었다. (the country's, big)

Animals _____ _____ _____ _____ _____ were

dying.

02 그들은 물을 가져다 주기 위해 수로를 지었다. (build, a canal, bring)

They _____ _____ _____ _____ _____ water.

03 운하는 흔히 배로 물건을 운반하는 데 사용된다. (often, use, transport)

Canals _____ _____ _____ _____ _____ goods

on boats.

04 이라크군과 미군은 동물들을 돕기 위해 함께 일했다. (work, help)

Iraqi and US soldiers _____ _____ _____ _____ the

animals.

05 그들은 탈출했던 동물들을 찾았다. (that, have, escape)

They searched for _____ _____ _____ _____.

A   영어 단어에는 우리말 뜻을, 우리말 뜻에는 영어 단어를 쓰시오.

01 share _____

02 consider _____

03 sale _____

04 win-win _____

05 concept _____

06 strike _____

07 _____ ~에 투표하다

08 _____ 상황

09 _____ 수천의

10 _____ 속담

11 _____ 받다

12 _____ 철, 쇠

B   굵게 표시된 부분에 유의하여 우리말 문장을 완성하시오.

01 Two people can think of **twice as many ideas as** one person can.

두 사람이 한 사람이 할 수 있는 것보다 _____ 생각해 낼 수 있다.

02 They have a special website **called LEGO Ideas**.

그들은 _____ 특별한 웹사이트를 갖고 있다.

03 **Anyone can share** ideas for new products on this site.

_____ 이 사이트에서 새로운 제품에 대한 아이디어를 _____.

04 **If they choose it**, it will become a real toy.

_____ 그것은 실제 장난감이 된다.

05 **The person who created the product** receives a little money from each sale.

_____ 판매 한 건당 약간의 돈을 받는다.

06 LEGO **gets thousands of free ideas** for new toys.

LEGO는 새로운 장난감에 대한 _____.

A 영어 단어에는 우리말 뜻을, 우리말 뜻에는 영어 단어를 쓰시오.

01 confuse _____

02 crash into _____

03 security _____

04 get lost _____

05 save _____

06 billions of _____

07 _____ 불필요한

08 _____ 따라가다

09 _____ 권장하다, 장려하다

10 _____ ~을 끄다

11 _____ 목적

12 _____ (동물이 계절을 따라) 이동하다

B 굵게 표시된 부분에 유의하여 우리말 문장을 완성하시오.

01 Do they do it **just to save energy**?

그들이 _____ 그렇게 할까?

02 They find their way **by following the stars**.

그들은 _____ 자신의 길을 찾는다.

03 Lights Out campaigns **are designed to help** these birds.

소등 캠페인은 이러한 새들을 _____.

04 People and companies **are encouraged to turn off** all unnecessary lights.

사람들과 기업들은 모든 불필요한 전등을 _____.

05 They can be covered **to make them less bright**.

_____ 그것들은 (덮개가) 씌워질 수도 있다.

06 Going dark this way **not only protects birds but also saves energy**.

이런 식으로 어두워지는 것은 _____.

A 주어진 우리말과 같은 뜻이 되도록 빈칸에 알맞은 말을 | 보기 |에서 골라 쓰시오. (필요시 형태 바꾸기)

| 보기 | clue   poorly   suspect   athlete   case

01 홈스가 한번은 그리스어 시험 문제 도난 사건을 해결한 적이 있다.

Holmes once solved a _____ of stolen Greek test questions.

02 세 명의 용의자들이 있었다.

There were three _____.

03 첫 번째 용의자는 육상 선수였다.

The first one was a(n) _____.

04 세 번째 용의자는 그 과목을 잘하지 못했다.

The third one did _____ in the subject.

05 홈스는 두 개의 단서들을 발견했는데, (그 단서는) 긁힌 자국과 흙이었다.

Holmes discovered two _____: scratches and dirt.

B 우리말 문장을 보고 주어진 영어 단어를 이용하여 문장을 완성하시오.

01 셜록 홈스는 어려운 문제들을 해결하는 것으로 유명하다. (famous, solve)

Sherlock Holmes _____ _____ _____ _____ difficult problems.

02 그는 결론들에 이르기 위해 작은 세부 사항들을 이용했다. (reach, conclusion)

He used small details _____ _____ _____.

03 이것들에 근거해 그는 (문제를 훔친) 도둑이 육상 선수라는 것을 알아차렸다. (base)

_____ _____ _____, he realized that the thief was the athlete.

04 그것들 사이로부터 흙이 떨어져 나왔다! (dirt, fall, from)

The _____ _____ _____ _____ between them!

05 만약 당신이 그렇게 한다면, 작지만 중요한 것들을 알아차릴 수 있을 것이다. (do)

_____ _____ _____, you'll notice little but important things.

A 주어진 우리말과 같은 뜻이 되도록 빈칸에 알맞은 말을 | 보기 |에서 골라 쓰시오. (필요시 형태 바꾸기)

| 보기 | alone   recipe   pickled   merchant   invention

01 미국에서만 매년 수백만 톤의 케첩이 팔린다.

In the US _____, millions of tons of ketchup are sold every year.

02 케첩은 미국의 발명품이 아니다.

Ketchup is not an American _____.

03 최초의 케첩은 원래 절인 생선이 들어 있었다.

The first ketchup originally contained _____ fish.

04 영국 상인들이 그것을 유럽으로 가지고 돌아갔다.

British _____ brought it back to Europe.

05 식품 회사들은 그의 조리법에 설탕과 식초를 추가했다.

Food companies added sugar and vinegar to his _____.

B 우리말 문장을 보고 주어진 영어 단어를 이용하여 문장을 완성하시오.

01 케첩은 세계에서 가장 인기 있는 소스 중 하나가 되었다. (popular)

Ketchup has become _____ _____ _____ _____ sauces in the world.

02 베트남 상인들이 중국에 그 소스를 들여왔다. (introduce, sauce)

Vietnamese traders _____ _____ _____ _____ China.

03 그것은 '케첩'이라고 불렸는데, 그것은 '생선 소스'를 의미한다. (mean, "fish sauce")

It was called "keh-jup," _____ _____ _____.

04 그들은 현지 음식을 추가함으로써 그 소스를 자신들의 입맛에 맞췄다. (add, foods)

They adapted the sauce to their taste _____ _____ _____ _____.

05 마침내 그 소스는 오늘날 우리가 아는 케첩이 되었다. (recognize)

The sauce became the ketchup _____ _____ today.

A 영어 단어에는 우리말 뜻을, 우리말 뜻에는 영어 단어를 쓰시오.

01 wrap _____   09 _____ 갈대

02 according to _____   10 _____ 함께 쓰다, 공유하다

03 improve _____   11 _____ 바르다

04 royalty _____   12 _____ 고대의

05 historian _____   13 _____ (물 위에) 뜨다

06 material _____   14 _____ 피하다

07 straw _____   15 _____ (접착제로) 붙이다

08 Egyptian _____   16 _____ 발명하다

B 굵게 표시된 부분에 유의하여 우리말 문장을 완성하시오.

01 **It is often said that** Marvin Stone invented the drinking straw.

_____ Marvin Stone이 빨대를 발명했다_____.

02 Ancient Egyptians **used straws to drink beer**.

고대 이집트인들은 _____.

03 They did so **to avoid drinking material** floating in the beer.

그들은 맥주에 떠다니는 _____ 그렇게 했다.

04 Beer has been **one of the most popular drinks** in the world.

맥주는 세계에서 _____였다.

05 They used **straws made of gold**!

그들은 _____ 사용했다!

06 He improved his design **by covering the paper in wax**.

그는 _____ 디자인을 개선했다.

A 영어 단어에는 우리말 뜻을, 우리말 뜻에는 영어 단어를 쓰시오.

01 joyful _____   07 _____ 행진하다

02 disappear _____   08 _____ 타당한

03 though _____   09 _____ 노예

04 homeland _____   10 _____ 죽음

05 express _____   11 _____ 장례식

06 soul _____   12 _____ 기념하다, 축하하다

B 굵게 표시된 부분에 유의하여 우리말 문장을 완성하시오.

01 You can **see marching jazz bands playing joyful music** during funerals.

당신은 장례식 동안 _____ 수 있다.

02 This **might seem strange**.

이것은 _____.

03 Africans **were brought to New Orleans** hundreds of years ago.

아프리카인들이 수백 년 전에 _____.

04 In their free time, they used music **to express their feelings**.

여가 시간에 그들은 _____ 음악을 이용했다.

05 Death would **free them from their hard lives**.

죽음이 _____.

06 **That's why people celebrate** with cheerful jazz music at funerals.

_____ 장례식에서 쾌활한 재즈 음악으로 _____.

A 주어진 우리말과 같은 뜻이 되도록 빈칸에 알맞은 말을 | 보기 |에서 골라 쓰시오. (필요시 형태 바꾸기)

| 보기 | soldier   across   source   poisonous   precious

01 감자는 세계 주요 식량원들 중 하나이다.

Potatoes are one of the world's major _____ of food.

02 다른 사람들은 그 식물의 독이 있는 꽃을 무서워했다.

Other people were scared of the plant's _____ flowers.

03 왕은 병사들에게 자신의 정원에 감자를 심으라고 시켰다.

The king told his _____ to plant potatoes in his garden.

04 이는 사람들이 감자가 귀중하다고 생각하게 만들었다.

This made people think the potatoes were _____.

05 감자는 유럽 전역에서 인기를 얻었다.

Potatoes became popular _____ Europe.

B 우리말 문장을 보고 주어진 영어 단어를 이용하여 문장을 완성하시오.

01 감자는 더운 날씨에 잘 자라는 것으로 보였다. (seem, grow)

Potatoes _____ _____ _____ in hot weather.

02 그들은 그것들을 요리하는 방법을 몰랐다. (how, cook)

They did not know _____ _____ _____ _____.

03 이것은 그들에게 심한 복통을 일으켰다. (cause, have)

This _____ _____ _____ _____ serious stomachaches.

04 그는 그 병사들에게 그것들을 지켜보라고 명령했다. (order, soldiers, watch over)

He _____ _____ _____ _____ _____ _____

them.

05 사람들은 직접 감자를 재배하기 시작했다. (start, grow, themselves)

People _____ _____ _____ _____.

A 주어진 우리말과 같은 뜻이 되도록 빈칸에 알맞은 말을 | 보기 |에서 골라 쓰시오. (필요시 형태 바꾸기)

| 보기 | envy   upset   proud   legend   branch

01 잎이 없어서, 그 나무의 나뭇가지들은 뿌리처럼 보인다.

Without leaves, the tree's _____ look like roots.

02 심지어 이 이상하게 생긴 나무에 관한 전설들도 있다.

There are even _____ about this strange-looking tree.

03 바오밥 나무는 그것을 알고 있었기 때문에 매우 거만했다.

Because the baobab knew that, it was very _____.

04 이는 신을 화나게 했다.

This made God _____.

05 바오밥 나무는 그것들을 부러워했다.

The baobab tree _____ them.

B 우리말 문장을 보고 주어진 영어 단어를 이용하여 문장을 완성하시오.

01 바오밥 나무는 아프리카에서 발견되는 이상하게 생긴 나무이다. (find, Africa)

The baobab tree is a strange-looking tree _____ _____ _____.

02 바오밥 나무는 '거꾸로 뒤집힌 나무'라는 별명으로 알려져 있다. (know, the nickname)

The baobab tree _____ _____ _____ _____

"upside-down tree."

03 신은 바오밥 나무를 세상에서 가장 강한 나무로 창조했다. (as, strong)

God created the baobab _____ _____ _____ _____ in the

world.

04 그것은 자신이 얼마나 위대한지를 모두에게 보여 주려고 노력했다. (try, show)

It _____ _____ _____ _____ how great it was.

05 신은 그것을 벌주기 위해 그것을 거꾸로 다시 심어버렸다. (punish)

God replanted it upside down _____ _____ _____.

A 영어 단어에는 우리말 뜻을, 우리말 뜻에는 영어 단어를 쓰시오.

01 mystery ＿＿＿＿＿＿＿

02 happen ＿＿＿＿＿＿＿

03 impact ＿＿＿＿＿＿＿

04 force ＿＿＿＿＿＿＿

05 untied ＿＿＿＿＿＿＿

06 put on ＿＿＿＿＿＿＿

07 pull on ＿＿＿＿＿＿＿

08 film ＿＿＿＿＿＿＿

09 ＿＿＿＿＿＿＿ 느슨해지다, 풀리다

10 ＿＿＿＿＿＿＿ 단단히, 꽉

11 ＿＿＿＿＿＿＿ 신발 끈

12 ＿＿＿＿＿＿＿ 흔들리다

13 ＿＿＿＿＿＿＿ (매듭을) 묶다, 매다

14 ＿＿＿＿＿＿＿ 신축성이 있다

15 ＿＿＿＿＿＿＿ 매듭

B 굵게 표시된 부분에 유의하여 우리말 문장을 완성하시오.

01 Researchers used a high-speed camera **to film the shoelaces**.

연구자들은 ＿＿＿＿＿＿＿＿＿＿＿＿＿＿＿＿＿＿＿ 고속 카메라를 사용했다.

02 For a long time, the shoelaces **stayed tightly tied**.

오랜 시간 동안 신발 끈은 ＿＿＿＿＿＿＿＿＿＿＿＿＿＿＿＿＿.

03 The first reason is **the force of a person's foot hitting the ground**.

첫 번째 이유는 ＿＿＿＿＿＿＿＿＿＿＿＿＿＿＿＿＿이다.

04 This impact **causes the knots in the shoelaces to loosen**.

이 충격은 ＿＿＿＿＿＿＿＿＿＿＿＿＿＿＿＿＿.

05 There are a few ways **to prevent the shoelaces from untying**.

＿＿＿＿＿＿＿＿＿＿＿＿＿＿＿＿＿ 몇 가지 방법이 있다.

06 As they shake, they pull on the knot, **slowly untying it**.

그것들이 흔들리면서, 매듭을 잡아당겨 ＿＿＿＿＿＿＿＿＿＿＿＿＿＿＿.

A 영어 단어에는 우리말 뜻을, 우리말 뜻에는 영어 단어를 쓰시오.

01 surface _____

02 volcanic _____

03 Jupiter _____

04 eruption _____

05 hundreds of _____

06 interestingly _____

07 _____ 화산

08 _____ 위성

09 _____ 암석

10 _____ 과정

11 _____ 행성

12 _____ 정반대의

B 굵게 표시된 부분에 유의하여 우리말 문장을 완성하시오.

01 It is called Io, and it's **Jupiter's third largest moon**.

그것은 Io라고 불리며, _____이다.

02 It orbits the planet **closer than the two larger moons**.

그것은 _____ 그 행성의 궤도를 돌고 있다.

03 This creates heat inside Io and **melts the rock inside it**.

이것은 Io 내부에 열을 만들어 내어 _____.

04 Over time, this process **has created more and more volcanoes** on Io.

시간이 지남에 따라, 이 과정은 Io에 _____.

05 Some of them **are bigger than Mount Everest**!

그들 중 일부는 _____!

A 주어진 우리말과 같은 뜻이 되도록 빈칸에 알맞은 말을 | 보기 |에서 골라 쓰시오. (필요시 형태 바꾸기)

| 보기 |　　cloth　　　spread　　　damage　　　protect　　　additional

01 화상 부위 위로 찬물을 흐르게 하고 깨끗한 천으로 감싸도록 한다.

Run cold water over the burn and cover it with a clean _____ .

02 이것은 공기로부터 그것을 보호하여 그것을 덜 아프게 한다.

This _____ it from the air so it hurts less.

03 그것들은 피부에 추가적인 손상을 야기할 수 있다.

They can cause further _____ to the skin.

04 먼저 더 물리는 것을 피하기 위해 그 사람을 뱀으로부터 떨어뜨려 놓는다.

First, get the person away from the snake to avoid _____ bites.

05 이것은 독이 퍼지는 것을 늦출 것이다.

This will slow down the _____ of the venom.

B 우리말 문장을 보고 주어진 영어 단어를 이용하여 문장을 완성하시오.

01 여기 가능한 상황에 대한 몇 가지 조언들이 있다. (tip, for)

_____ _____ _____ _____ _____ possible situations.

02 그들은 자신의 몸을 가만히 두어야 한다. (keep, very still)

They should _____ _____ _____ _____ _____ .

03 공황 상태는 그들의 심박동수를 증가하게 할 수 있다. (cause, heart rate)

Panic can _____ _____ _____ _____ _____ increase.

04 상처 부위를 비누와 물로 씻어라. (soap)

Wash the affected area _____ _____ _____ .

05 그 사람이 숨 쉬기 어려워하면, 의사에게 데리고 가라. (difficulty, breathe)

If the person _____ _____ _____ , take them to a doctor.

A 주어진 우리말과 같은 뜻이 되도록 빈칸에 알맞은 말을 | 보기 |에서 골라 쓰시오. (필요시 형태 바꾸기)

| 보기 | focus on   anxiety   compare   suffer from   stand for

01 FOMO는 '놓치는 것에 대한 두려움'을 의미한다.

FOMO _____ the "fear of missing out."

02 그것은 당신이 사교 모임에서 소외되는 것과 같은 불안감을 말한다.

It refers to the _____ of feeling like you're missing out on a social event.

03 그들은 자신의 삶을 또래들의 삶과 비교한다.

They _____ their own lives to the ones of their peers.

04 JOMO를 겪는 사람들은 자신에게 집중한다.

People with JOMO _____ themselves.

05 당신은 FOMO로 고생하고 있는가?

Do you _____ FOMO?

B 우리말 문장을 보고 주어진 영어 단어를 이용하여 문장을 완성하시오.

01 그들은 자신의 삶에 만족한다. (satisfied with)

They _____ _____ _____ _____ _____.

02 그들은 자신이 실제로 좋아하는 사람들하고만 관계를 맺는 경향이 있다. (tend, relationships)

They _____ _____ _____ _____ only with people they actually like.

03 당신이 모든 사교 모임에 참석할 필요는 없다. (need, attend)

You _____ _____ _____ _____ every social event.

04 이것은 당신이 (스마트) 기기로부터 잠시 쉬는 것을 포함한다. (involve, take)

_____ _____ _____ a break from your devices.

05 당신은 자신의 삶에 더 집중할 수 있을 것이다. (able, focus)

You'll _____ _____ _____ _____ more on your life.

A 영어 단어에는 우리말 뜻을, 우리말 뜻에는 영어 단어를 쓰시오.

01 pick _____   07 _____ 냉장고

02 soil _____   08 _____ 운송하다

03 save _____   09 _____ 산소

04 instead of _____   10 _____ ~라면 어떻게 될까?

05 taste _____   11 _____ 먼 곳으로부터

06 shopper _____

B 굵게 표시된 부분에 유의하여 우리말 문장을 완성하시오.

01 They taste best **when you pick them yourself**.

_____ 가장 맛이 좋다.

02 **What if you don't have** your own garden?

_____ 자신의 정원을 _____?

03 **That's because there is a vegetable garden** inside the Metro supermarket.

Metro 슈퍼마켓 안에 _____.

04 The garden **looks like** a supermarket refrigerator.

그 정원은 슈퍼마켓의 냉장고_____.

05 The soil **helps the plants grow**.

이 흙은 _____.

06 It **doesn't have to transport** vegetables from far away.

그것은 먼 곳에서 채소를 _____.

A 영어 단어에는 우리말 뜻을, 우리말 뜻에는 영어 단어를 쓰시오.

01 dizziness	_____	09 _____	부작용
02 period	_____	10 _____	창백한
03 juice	_____	11 _____	실명
04 lead	_____	12 _____	독성이 있는
05 cosmetics	_____	13 _____	~동안 쭉, 내내
06 fashionable	_____	14 _____	생명을 앗아갈, 치명적인
07 lead to	_____	15 _____	재료, 성분
08 vision	_____	16 _____	자주

B 굵게 표시된 부분에 유의하여 우리말 문장을 완성하시오.

01 Throughout history, many cultures **have used cosmetics**.

역사를 통틀어 많은 문화권에서 _____.

02 Many cosmetics **used to contain** lead, which is poisonous.

많은 화장품에 납이 _____, 그것에는 독성이 있다.

03 It was fashionable for women **to have very pale skin**.

여자들이 _____ 유행했다.

04 **After using it regularly**, many women suffered from serious side effects.

_____, 많은 여성들이 심각한 부작용에 시달렸다.

05 European women used the juice from this plant **to make their pupils bigger**.

유럽 여성들은 _____ 이 식물로부터 나온 즙을 사용했다.

06 Thankfully, cosmetics **are much safer** today.

다행히 오늘날 화장품은 _____.

A 주어진 우리말과 같은 뜻이 되도록 빈칸에 알맞은 말을 | 보기 |에서 골라 쓰시오. (필요시 형태 바꾸기)

| 보기 | 　huge　　trash　　strategy　　seriousness　　produce

01 그는 사람들의 관심을 얻기 위해서 특별한 전략을 이용했다.

He used a special _____ to get people's attention.

02 그는 한 달 동안 진짜 쓰레기를 입은 것이다!

He wore real _____ for a month!

03 그는 환경 문제의 심각성을 깨닫게 되었다.

He realized the _____ of environmental problems.

04 대부분의 사람들이 자신이 얼마나 많은 쓰레기를 만들어 내는지 모른다.

Most people don't know how much waste they _____.

05 사람들이 작은 변화를 만들기만 하면, 큰 차이를 가져올 수 있다.

It could make a(n) _____ difference if people just make small changes.

B 우리말 문장을 보고 주어진 영어 단어를 이용하여 문장을 완성하시오.

01 Greenfield가 항상 운동가였던 것은 아니었다. (always)

Greenfield _____ _____ an activist.

02 그는 쓰레기를 입기로 결심했다. (decide, wear)

_____ _____ _____ _____ trash.

03 (과거에) 그는 돈을 버는 데 집중했었다. (used, focused)

He _____ _____ _____ _____ on making money.

04 그는 한 달 동안 그가 만들어 낸 모든 쓰레기 조각을 넣었다. (piece, trash)

He added _____ _____ _____ _____ that he produced for a month.

05 그는 사람들이 자신이 만들어 내는 쓰레기에 대해 생각하게 되기를 바랐다. (hope, think)

He _____ _____ _____ _____ _____ the waste they produce.

본책 p. 82   이름

A 주어진 우리말과 같은 뜻이 되도록 빈칸에 알맞은 말을 | 보기 |에서 골라 쓰시오. (필요시 형태 바꾸기)

| 보기 | major   instead   several   confused   forecaster

01 한 나라에 두 개의 태풍이 동시에 오면, 사람들은 혼란스러워했다.

When a country had two typhoons at the same time, people got _____.

02 처음에 일기 예보관들은 실제 사람의 이름을 따서 태풍의 이름을 지었다.

At first, weather _____ named typhoons after real people.

03 매해 여름마다 주요 태풍들이 있다.

There are _____ typhoons every summer.

04 몇몇 나라들은 태풍에 붙일 140개의 이름 목록을 만들었다.

_____ countries have made a list of 140 names for typhoons.

05 대신에 그들은 새 이름을 선정한다.

They choose a new name _____.

B 우리말 문장을 보고 주어진 영어 단어를 이용하여 문장을 완성하시오.

01 1800년대 후반까지, 태풍에 이름이 부여되지 않았다. (give, names)

Until the late 1800s, typhoons _____ _____ _____ _____.

02 그들은 자신들이 좋아하지 않는 유명한 사람들의 이름을 따서 태풍의 이름을 지었다. (like)

They named them after famous _____ _____ _____ _____.

03 그것은 점점 더 약해지고 있다. (weaker)

It is becoming _____ _____ _____.

04 오늘날 태풍은 다른 많은 것들의 이름을 따서 지어진다. (name)

Today, typhoons _____ _____ _____ many other things.

05 그 이름들은 하나씩 차례로 쓰인다. (one)

The names are used _____ _____ _____.

A 영어 단어에는 우리말 뜻을, 우리말 뜻에는 영어 단어를 쓰시오.

01	act	_____	**08**	_____ ~을 알아채다
02	weak	_____	**09**	_____ ~을 통해
03	far away	_____	**10**	_____ 능력
04	amount	_____	**11**	_____ (액체의) 방울
05	huge	_____	**12**	_____ 강력한
06	human	_____	**13**	_____ 감각; 느끼다, 감지하다
07	seawater	_____	**14**	_____ (~의 위치를) 찾아내다

B 굵게 표시된 부분에 유의하여 우리말 문장을 완성하시오.

01 These openings act **much in the same way as our noses do**.

이 구멍은 _____ 기능한다.

02 Some fish have a sense of smell that is **500 times more powerful than** a human's!

어떤 물고기들은 인간의 후각_____ 후각을 가지고 있다!

03 This strong sense of smell **helps fish locate food**.

이 강력한 후각은 _____.

04 Fish can pick up **even very weak smells** in the water.

물고기는 물속의 _____ 감지해 낼 수 있다.

05 **There is only one drop of blood** in a huge amount of seawater.

엄청난 양의 바닷물 속에 _____.

06 The sense of smell is **one of a fish's most important abilities**.

후각은 _____이다.

A 영어 단어에는 우리말 뜻을, 우리말 뜻에는 영어 단어를 쓰시오.

01 college _____

02 wheelchair _____

03 static _____

04 sign _____

05 disability _____

06 strengthen _____

07 parking space _____

08 officially _____

09 _____ 활동적인

10 _____ 채택하다

11 _____ 특징으로 삼다

12 _____ 수동적인

13 _____ 상징(물)

14 _____ 도구

15 _____ 교수

16 _____ 인식, 지각

B 굵게 표시된 부분에 유의하여 우리말 문장을 완성하시오.

01 Are there any signs **that you would like to change**?

_____ 표지판이 있는가?

02 The symbol in the old sign **was too static**.

그 오래된 표지판 속 상징이 _____.

03 They wanted people **to view wheelchairs simply as tools**.

그들은 사람들이 _____ 바랐다.

04 They created a new design **featuring a person in a moving wheelchair**.

그들은 _____ 새로운 디자인을 만들어냈다.

05 They **started putting** stickers with the new design.

그들은 새로운 디자인으로 된 스티커를 _____.

06 The sign would change **people's perceptions of people with disabilities**.

그 표지판이 _____ 변화시킬 것이다.

A 주어진 우리말과 같은 뜻이 되도록 빈칸에 알맞은 말을 | 보기 |에서 골라 쓰시오. (필요시 형태 바꾸기)

| 보기 | collect   purpose   carry   donate   fall off

01 많은 아이들이 어디든지 갖고 다니는 가장 좋아하는 장난감을 가지고 있다.

Many children have a favorite toy that they _____ everywhere.

02 눈은 사라지고 팔은 떨어진다.

Eyes get lost, and arms _____.

03 그들은 기부를 통해 낡은 장난감들을 수집했다.

They _____ old toys through donations.

04 그 캠페인은 또한 더 진지한 목적이 있었다.

The campaign also had a more serious _____.

05 일본에는 장기 기증을 하는 사람들이 충분하지 않다.

Not enough people in Japan _____ organs.

B 우리말 문장을 보고 주어진 영어 단어를 이용하여 문장을 완성하시오.

01 시간이 지날수록 이 장난감은 너덜너덜해지기 시작한다. (begin, fall)

Over time, these toys _____ _____ _____ _____.

02 두 명의 직원이 이러한 장난감들을 고치는 캠페인을 시작했다. (a campaign, fix)

Two workers started _____ _____ _____ _____ these toys.

03 그 기부받은 장난감들의 부품으로 아이들의 장난감들을 고쳤다. (donate, toy)

They fixed the children's toys with parts from _____ _____ _____.

04 그 캠페인은 사람들이 이 문제를 알게 하기를 원했다. (make, aware)

The campaign wanted to _____ _____ _____ _____ this problem.

05 그것은 장기 기증의 중요성에 대한 의식을 높이는 데 성공했다. (increase, awareness)

It succeeded in _____ _____ _____ the importance of organ donations.

A 주어진 우리말과 같은 뜻이 되도록 빈칸에 알맞은 말을 | 보기 |에서 골라 쓰시오. (필요시 형태 바꾸기)

	보기	hit control sense average gap

01 그것이 머리에 닿자 매우 차갑게 느껴진다.

When it _____ your head, it feels very cold.

02 이 점들은 외부의 온도를 감지한다.

These spots _____ the outside temperature.

03 이 점들은 당신의 피부 온도 변화를 조절한다.

These spots _____ changes in your skin's temperature.

04 사람 손의 평균 온도는 섭씨 31도이다.

The _____ temperature of a person's hands is 31 degrees Celsius.

05 추운 날에는 이 격차가 훨씬 더 커진다.

On a cold day, this _____ becomes even bigger.

B 우리말 문장을 보고 주어진 영어 단어를 이용하여 문장을 완성하시오.

01 어느 추운 날 당신은 막 머리를 감으려고 한다. (about, wash)

You _____ _____ _____ _____ your hair on a cold day.

02 당신이 손으로 물을 만졌을 때 그것이 따뜻하게 느껴진다. (feel)

When you touch the water with your hand, _____ _____ _____.

03 그것은 당신이 피부에 냉점과 온점을 가지고 있기 때문이다. (it)

_____ _____ you have cold and warm spots on your skin.

04 같은 외부 온도도 따뜻하거나 차갑게 느껴질 수 있다. (either)

The same outside temperature can feel _____ _____ _____

_____.

05 당신의 손이 당신의 머리보다 더 빨리 차가워진다. (quickly, do)

Your hands get colder _____ _____ _____ _____

_____ _____.

A 영어 단어에는 우리말 뜻을, 우리말 뜻에는 영어 단어를 쓰시오.

01 over _____

02 identify _____

03 influence _____

04 matching _____

05 annual _____

06 instead of _____

07 unique _____

08 _____ 인쇄업자

09 _____ 정확한

10 _____ 산업

11 _____ 지정하다

12 _____ 단색

13 _____ 화장품

14 _____ 무수한, 셀 수 없이 많은

B 굵게 표시된 부분에 유의하여 우리말 문장을 완성하시오.

01 There is a company **that designates one special color** each year.

매년 _____ 한 회사가 있다.

02 Pantone **is known for** its color matching system.

Pantone은 색상을 매칭해 주는 시스템_____.

03 The company **has identified** over 2,000 different solid colors.

이 회사는 2천여 가지가 넘는 서로 다른 단색을 _____.

04 Each color **has been given** its own unique number.

각각의 색상에는 고유의 번호가 _____.

05 This system **is very helpful** for other prefessionals.

이 시스템은 다른 전문가들에게 _____.

06 **Instead of calling a color "dark red,"** they can call it "19-1664."

_____ 그들은 그것을 '19-1664'라고 부를 수 있다.

07 This **allows everyone to know** the exact color.

이것은 정확한 색상을 _____.

38

본책 p. 99   이름

A 영어 단어에는 우리말 뜻을, 우리말 뜻에는 영어 단어를 쓰시오.

01 eventually ＿＿＿＿＿＿＿＿＿   09 ＿＿＿＿＿＿＿＿＿ 공무원

02 hillside ＿＿＿＿＿＿＿＿＿   10 ＿＿＿＿＿＿＿＿＿ 건설, 공사

03 add ＿＿＿＿＿＿＿＿＿   11 ＿＿＿＿＿＿＿＿＿ 거주자, 주민

04 outdoor ＿＿＿＿＿＿＿＿＿   12 ＿＿＿＿＿＿＿＿＿ 해결책

05 roof ＿＿＿＿＿＿＿＿＿   13 ＿＿＿＿＿＿＿＿＿ 가파른

06 section ＿＿＿＿＿＿＿＿＿   14 ＿＿＿＿＿＿＿＿＿ 이동하다

07 located ＿＿＿＿＿＿＿＿＿   15 ＿＿＿＿＿＿＿＿＿ 무료의

08 protect ＿＿＿＿＿＿＿＿＿   16 ＿＿＿＿＿＿＿＿＿ 보다 나은 쪽으로

B 굵게 표시된 부분에 유의하여 우리말 문장을 완성하시오.

01 It **is located on** a steep hillside.

그것은 가파른 언덕 비탈＿＿＿＿＿＿＿＿＿＿＿＿＿＿＿＿＿＿＿＿＿＿＿＿＿＿.

02 Many Comuna 13 residents **had to climb** hundreds of steps every day.

많은 Comuna 13 주민들은 매일 수백 개의 계단을 ＿＿＿＿＿＿＿＿＿＿＿＿＿＿＿.

03 This useful escalator **is free to ride**.

이 유용한 에스컬레이터는 ＿＿＿＿＿＿＿＿＿＿＿＿＿＿＿＿＿＿＿＿＿＿＿.

04 Before it was built, **it took 35 minutes to walk** to the top.

그것이 지어지기 전에는 정상까지 ＿＿＿＿＿＿＿＿＿＿＿＿＿＿＿＿＿＿＿＿.

05 It's possible **to do so in six minutes**.

＿＿＿＿＿＿＿＿＿＿＿＿＿＿＿＿＿＿＿＿＿＿＿＿＿＿＿＿＿ 가능하다.

06 **People using the escalator** weren't protected from the rain or hot sun.

＿＿＿＿＿＿＿＿＿＿＿＿＿＿＿＿＿＿＿＿ 비 혹은 뜨거운 햇빛으로부터 보호받지 못했다.

A 주어진 우리말과 같은 뜻이 되도록 빈칸에 알맞은 말을 | 보기 |에서 골라 쓰시오. (필요시 형태 바꾸기)

| 보기 |　　　release　　　below　　　spread　　　volcanic　　　benefit

01 화산 폭발이 많은 이점을 갖고 있다는 것을 알았는가?

Did you know that _____ eruptions have many benefits?

02 화산이 폭발하면 공기 중으로 재를 내뿜는다.

When a volcano erupts, it _____ ash into the air.

03 재는 화산 주변 지역으로 퍼진다.

The ash _____ to areas around the volcano.

04 화산의 또 다른 이점은 그것이 많은 에너지를 생산한다는 것이다.

Another _____ of volcanoes is that they produce a lot of energy.

05 열이 지면 아래에 있으면, 온천이 만들어지는 데 도움이 된다.

When the heat is _____ ground, it helps to create hot springs.

B 우리말 문장을 보고 주어진 영어 단어를 이용하여 문장을 완성하시오.

01 재에서 발견되는 영양분은 식물이 자라도록 돕는다. (plants, grow)

The nutrients found in ash _____ _____ _____.

02 농부들은 휴화산 주변에 사는 것을 선호한다. (like, live)

Farmers _____ _____ _____ near dormant volcanoes.

03 많은 나라들이 심지어 전기를 만들기 위해 화산 에너지를 사용하기 시작했다. (make, electricity)

Many countries have even begun to use volcanic energy _____ _____

_____.

04 화산이 지구의 공기와 물의 대부분을 만들어 왔다. (produce)

Volcanoes _____ _____ most of the Earth's air and water.

05 화산은 우리가 지구상에 사는 것을 가능하게 해 준다! (us, live)

Volcanoes make it possible _____ _____ _____ _____

on Earth!

A 주어진 우리말과 같은 뜻이 되도록 빈칸에 알맞은 말을 |보기|에서 골라 쓰시오. (필요시 형태 바꾸기)

|보기|	available	worth	charge	pollute	opinion

01 여기 전기차에 관한 저희의 의견들이 있어요.

Here are our _____ about electric cars.

02 그것들은 충전하기가 아주 쉬워요.

They are very easy to _____.

03 휘발유 자동차와 달리 전기차는 공기를 오염시키지 않아요.

Unlike gas-powered cars, electric cars don't _____ the air.

04 이용 가능한 충전소가 많이 없어요.

There aren't many charging stations _____.

05 40~45마일 어치의 전기를 전기차에 넣는 데 약 한 시간이나 걸려요.

It takes about an hour to add 40 to 45 miles' _____ of electricity to an electric car.

B 우리말 문장을 보고 주어진 영어 단어를 이용하여 문장을 완성하시오.

01 Suzie는 새 차를 살 예정이에요. (going, buy)

Suzie _____ _____ _____ _____ a new car.

02 그것들은 휘발유 자동차만큼 소음을 많이 내지도 않아요. (much noise)

They don't make _____ _____ _____ _____ gas-powered cars.

03 그것들은 환경에 훨씬 이로워요. (much, good)

They are _____ _____ _____ the environment.

04 내가 장거리 자동차 여행을 할 때 그것이 문제가 될 수도 있어요. (go)

That might be a problem _____ _____ _____ _____ road trips.

05 전기차는 충전하는 데 오랜 시간이 걸려요. (take)

Electric cars _____ _____ _____ _____ _____ charge.

기초부터 내신까지 중학 독해 완성

1316

1316 READING

WORKBOOK
정답

LEVEL
2

B

01 무척 고요하고 평화로워 보일까
02 모든 것을 더 조용하게 만들기
03 이것을 가능하게 한다
04 눈이 녹으면서[녹을수록], 더 작아진다
05 소리를 더 크게 들리게 한다
06 눈이 녹기 시작하면[시작할 때]

Section 2 03
p. 8

A

01 symbol   02 letter   03 curved
04 customers   05 represent

B

01 what it is   02 looks like a smile
03 the largest pizza company
04 wanted to add a dot   05 changed its mind

Section 2 04
p. 9

A

01 ran   02 dish   03 tender
04 dough   05 flipped

B

01 worked as a chef   02 came up with
03 helped the apples absorb
04 richer and sweeter than ever
05 the moment, was born

Section 3 01
p. 10

A

01 미끄러운   02 토양, 흙   03 개울, 시내
04 녹이다   05 야기하다, 초래하다 06 전열선
07 흐르다   08 해를 끼치다, 손상시키다
09 harmless   10 contain   11 chemical
12 slide   13 volcanic   14 mineral

15 sidewalk   16 prevent

B

01 우리가 안전하게 인도 위를 걷게 해 준다
02 토양에 안 좋은
03 물고기에게 문제를 일으킬 수 있다
04 대안을 만들어 왔다   05 눈과 얼음을 녹일 수 있는
06 사람들과 자동차가, 미끄러지지 않게 해 준다

Section 3 02
p. 11

A

01 (값이) 싼   02 할인된   03 고객, 소비자
04 일어나다, 발생하다 05 ~보다 위에   06 결과적으로
07 받다   08 original   09 effect
10 imagine   11 expensive   12 experience
13 based on   14 in other words

B

01 당신이 쇼핑하러 가서, 찾았다고 상상해 봐라
02 방금, 경험하였다
03 자신들이 받은 첫 번째 정보에 근거하여
04 정가 위에 할인된 가격을
06 할인된 가격이 더 좋아 보이게 한다
07 살 가능성이 더 높다

Section 3 03
p. 12

A

01 uncommon   02 feathers   03 nutrients
04 remove   05 survive

B

01 both people and animals
02 can be affected by
03 which helps plants make
04 that turn brown in winter
05 allows them to get

Section 3 04
p. 13

A

01 stored   02 scenes   03 invented
04 observe   05 captured

B

01 were hard to carry   02 had to return to
03 tried to remember   04 Thanks to these tubes
05 one of the most famous impressionists

Section 4 01
p. 14

A

01 항공사   02 향기, 향내   03 분명히
04 특징, 특색   05 강력한   06 석쇠에 굽다
07 ~에 영향을 미치다   08 uniform
09 native   10 specific   11 memory
12 flight attendant 13 passenger   14 vent

B

01 고객들의 마음속에 머물기 위해
02 싱가포르가 원산지인   03 승무원 제복에 사용된다
04 냄새를 퍼뜨리기 위해
05 사람들이 배고픔을 느끼게 만든다[한다]
06 알게 되었다

Section 4 02
p. 15

A

01 정상적인   02 알아보다   03 아마
04 일상적인   05 자주   06 물건, 물체
07 function   08 useful   09 survive
10 take a look at   11 experience   12 sneak up

B

01 본 적이 있는가   02 사람들이, 얼굴을 보게 한다
03 우리가 생존하게 도와주었다[우리가 살아남도록 도왔다]
04 얼굴을 알아볼 수 있는 것은
05 우리의 적(들)이, 몰래 접근하는 것을 막았다
06 부분들을 합치려고 자주 애쓴다

Section 4 03
p. 16

A

01 modern   02 Unfortunately   03 drain
04 end up   05 absorb

B

01 are usually less than   02 help people feel cleaner
03 could be harmed by
04 banned companies from using
05 if they contain microbeads

Section 4 04
p. 17

A

01 immediately   02 empty   03 local
04 volunteered   05 organizations

B

01 in the country's biggest zoo
02 built a canal to bring
03 are often used to transport
04 worked together to help
05 animals that had escaped

Section 5 01
p. 18

A

01 공유하다   02 고려하다, 검토하다 03 판매
04 모두에게 유리한, 모두가 득을 보는
05 개념   06 때리다, 치다   07 vote for
08 situation   09 thousands of   10 old saying
11 receive   12 iron

B

01 두 배만큼 많은 아이디어를   02 LEGO Ideas라고 불리는
03 누구나, 공유할 수 있다   04 (만약) 그들이 그것을 선정하면
05 그 제품을 만든 사람은
06 수천 개의 공짜 아이디어를 얻는다

Section 5 02
p. 19

A

01 혼란시키다 02 ~와 충돌하다 03 보안, 치안
04 길을 잃다 05 절약하다 06 수십억의
07 unnecessary 08 follow 09 encourage
10 turn off 11 purpose 12 migrate

B

01 단지 에너지를 절약하기 위해서 02 별을 따라감으로써
03 돕기 위해 고안되었다 04 고도록 권장된다
05 그것들을 덜 밝게 만들기 위해
06 새들을 보호할 뿐만 아니라 에너지도 절약한다

Section 5 03
p. 20

A

01 case 02 suspects 03 athlete
04 poorly 05 clues

B

01 is famous for solving 02 to reach conclusions
03 Based on these 04 dirt fell out from
05 If you do

Section 5 04
p. 21

A

01 alone 02 invention 03 pickled
04 merchants 05 recipe

B

01 one of the most popular
02 introduced the sauce to
03 which means "fish sauce"
04 by adding local foods
05 we recognize

Section 6 01
p. 22

A

01 (포장지로) 싸다 02 ~에 따르면 03 개선하다
04 왕족 05 역사가 06 물질
07 빨대 08 이집트인 09 reed
10 share 11 cover 12 ancient
13 float 14 avoid 15 glue
16 invent

B

01 흔히, 고 전해진다[한다]
02 맥주를 마시기 위해 빨대를 사용했다
03 물질을 마시는 것을 피하기 위해
04 가장 인기 있는 음료 중 하나 05 금으로 만든 빨대를
06 종이에 왁스를 바름으로써

Section 6 02
p. 23

A

01 즐거운 02 사라지다 03 비록 ~이지만
04 고국, 모국 05 표현하다 06 영혼
07 march 08 good 09 slave
10 death 11 funeral 12 celebrate

B

01 행진하는 재즈 밴드가 즐거운 음악을 연주하는 것을 볼
02 이상하게 보일지 모른다
03 뉴올리언스로 건너오게 되었다
04 자신의 감정을 표현하기 위해
05 그들의 힘든 삶으로부터 그들을 자유롭게 해 주는 것이다
06 그것이 사람들이, 축하하는[기념하는] 이유이다

Section 6 03
p. 24

A

01 sources 02 poisonous 03 soldiers
04 precious 05 across

B

01 seemed to grow well 02 how to cook them

03 caused them to have
04 ordered the soldiers to watch over
05 started growing potatoes themselves

Section 6 04
p. 25

A

01 branches　　02 legends　　03 proud
04 upset　　05 envied

B

01 found in Africa
02 is known by[as] the nickname
03 as the strongest tree
04 tried to show everyone
05 to punish it

Section 7 01
p. 26

A

01 미스터리, 난제　02 일어나다, 생기다　03 충돌, 충격
04 힘　　05 묶이지 않은, 풀린　06 ~을 입다, 신다
07 ~을 잡아당기다　08 촬영하다, 찍다　09 loosen
10 tightly　　11 shoelace　　12 shake
13 tie　　14 stretch　　15 knot

B

01 신발 끈을 촬영하기 위해　02 꽉 묶인 채로 있었다
03 사람의 발이 땅에 부딪히는 힘
04 신발 끈의 매듭이 느슨해지게 한다
05 신발 끈이 풀리는 것을 막는　06 천천히 그것을 풀리게 한다

Section 7 02
p. 27

A

01 표면　　02 화산의　　03 목성
04 (화산의) 폭발, 분화　　05 수백의
06 흥미롭게도　07 volcano　　08 moon
09 rock　　10 process　　11 planet
12 opposite

B

01 목성의 세 번째로 큰 위성
02 두 개의 더 큰 위성보다 더 가까이
03 그 안에 있는 암석을 녹인다
04 점점 더 많은 화산을 만들어 왔다
05 에베레스트산보다 더 크다

Section 7 03
p. 28

A

01 cloth　　02 protects　　03 damage
04 additional　　05 spread

B

01 Here are some tips for
02 keep their body[bodies] very still
03 cause their heart rate to
04 with soap and water　05 has difficulty breathing

Section 7 04
p. 29

A

01 stands for　　02 anxiety　　03 compare
04 focus on　　05 suffer from

B

01 are satisfied with their lives
02 tend to have relationships
03 don't need to attend
04 This involves taking
05 be able to focus

Section 8 01
p. 30

A

01 (과일 등을) 따다　02 흙, 땅　　03 절약하다
04 ~ 대신에　　05 맛이 ~하다　　06 쇼핑객, 고객
07 refrigerator　　08 transport　　09 oxygen
10 what if ~?　　11 from far away

B

01 당신이 직접 그것들을 딸 때
02 당신이, 갖고 있지 않다면 어떨까
03 채소 정원이 있기 때문이다   04 처럼 생겼다
05 식물들이 자라도록 돕는다   06 운송해 올 필요가 없다

B

01 were not given names
02 people they didn't like
03 weaker and weaker
04 are named after   05 one by one

Section 8 02   p. 31

A

01 현기증, 어지럼증   02 기간, 시기   03 즙
04 납   05 화장품   06 유행하는
07 ~으로 이어지다   08 시력   09 side effect
10 pale   11 blindness   12 poisonous
13 throughout   14 deadly   15 ingredient
16 regularly

B

01 화장품을 사용해 왔다   02 들어 있곤 했는데
03 매우 창백한 피부를 갖는 것이
04 그것을 자주 사용한 후에
05 그들의 동공을 더 크게 만들기 위해
06 훨씬 더 안전하다

Section 9 01   p. 34

A

01 역할[기능]을 하다 02 약한, 희미한   03 멀리 (떨어져)
04 양   05 거대한, 막대한   06 인간
07 해수, 바닷물   08 pick up   09 through
10 ability   11 drop   12 powerful
13 sense   14 locate

B

01 우리의 코가 하는 것과 거의[매우] 같은 방식으로
02 보다 500배나 더 강력한
03 물고기가 음식의 위치를 찾는 데 도움을 준다
04 매우 희미한 냄새까지도
05 단 한 방울의 피가 있다
06 물고기의 가장 중요한 능력 중 하나

Section 8 03   p. 32

A

01 strategy   02 trash   03 seriousness
04 produce   05 huge

B

01 wasn't always   02 He decided to wear
03 used to be focused   05 every piece of trash
05 hoped that people would think

Section 9 02   p. 35

A

01 대학   02 휠체어   03 정적인
04 표지판   05 장애   06 강화하다
07 주차장   08 공식적으로, 정식으로
09 active   10 adopt   11 feature
12 passive   13 symbol   14 tool
15 professor   16 perception

B

01 당신이 바꾸고 싶은   02 너무 정적이었다
03 휠체어를 단순히 도구라고 여기길
04 움직이는 휠체어를 탄 사람을 특징으로 하는
05 붙이기 시작했다
06 장애인에 대한 사람들의 인식을

Section 8 04   p. 33

A

01 confused   02 forecasters   03 major
04 Several   05 instead

Section 9 `03`

p. 36

A

01 carry 02 fall off 03 collected
04 purpose 05 donate

B

01 begin to fall apart 02 a campaign to fix
03 the donated toys 04 make people aware of
05 increasing awareness about

Section 9 `04`

p. 37

A

01 hits 02 sense 03 control
04 average 05 gap

B

01 are about to wash 02 it feels warm
03 It's because 04 either warm or cold
05 more quickly than your head does

Section 10 `01`

p. 38

A

01 ~이 넘는 02 식별하다 03 영향을 미치다
04 어울리는, 조화되는 05 매년의 06 ~ 대신에
07 고유의, 독특한 08 printer 09 exact
10 industry 11 designate 12 solid color
13 cosmetics 14 countless

B

01 하나의 특별한 색상을 지정하는
02 으로 알려져 있다 03 식별해 왔다
04 부여되어 왔다 05 매우 도움이 된다
06 한 색상을 '검붉은색[어두운 붉은색]'이라 부르는 대신에
07 모든 사람이 알게 해 준다

Section 10 `02`

p. 39

A

01 마침내, 결국 02 (작은 산·언덕의) 비탈
03 추가하다 04 야외의 05 지붕
06 (시·군의) 구역 07 (~에) 위치한 08 보호하다
09 official 10 construction 11 resident
12 solution 13 steep 14 travel
15 free 16 for the better

B

01 에 위치해 있다 02 올라야 했다
03 탑승이 무료이다 04 걸어서 35분이 걸렸다
05 6분 만에 그렇게 하는 것이
06 에스컬레이터를 사용하는 사람들이

Section 10 `03`

p. 40

A

01 volcanic 02 releases 03 spreads
04 benefit 05 below

B

01 help plants grow 02 like to live
03 to make electricity 04 have produced
05 for us to live

Section 10 `04`

p. 41

A

01 opinions 02 charge 03 pollute
04 available 05 worth

B

01 is going to buy 02 as much noise as
03 much better for 04 when I go on
05 take a long time to

MEMO

MEMO

MEMO

MEMO

MEMO

MEMO